LOGGED IN AND STRESSED OUT

T0049259

LOGGED IN AND STRESSED OUT

How Social Media Is Affecting Your Mental Health and What You Can Do About It

Paula Durlofsky

ROWMAN & LITTLEFIELD
Lanham • Boulder • New York • London

Published by Rowman & Littlefield
An imprint of The Rowman & Littlefield Publishing Group, Inc.
4501 Forbes Boulevard, Suite 200, Lanham, Maryland 20706
www.rowman.com

86-90 Paul Street, London EC2A 4NE, United Kingdom

British Library Cataloguing in Publication Information Available

Library of Congress Cataloging-in-Publication Data

Names: Durlofsky, Paula, author.
Title: Logged in and stressed out : how social media is affecting your mental health and what you can do about it / Paula Durlofsky.
Description: Lanham : Rowman & Littlefield, 2020. | Includes bibliographical references and index.
Identifiers: LCCN 2020944931 (print) | ISBN 9781538126677 (hardcover) | ISBN 9781538176290 (paperback) | ISBN 9781538126684 (ebook)
Subjects: LCSH: Social media—Psychological aspects. | Digital media—Social aspects.| Mental health.
Classification: LCC LC HM742 .D875 2020 (print) | DDC 302.231
LC record available at https://lccn.loc.gov/2020944931

For my loving family—Larry, Sarah, and Hope

CONTENTS

ACKNOWLEDGMENTS

Soon after creating a Facebook account in 2009, I was hooked. Reconnecting with friends from my past with whom I'd lost contact has enhanced my life in ways I'd never imagined would have been possible. However, some time ago I began to become aware that sometimes I'd be logged in for too long—and not always for the best reasons. More and more in my therapy practice I started hearing my clients express concerns about how social media was affecting their lives and relationships. That's when the idea for writing this book came about.

Having the idea to write a book and actually doing it is as great a leap as it sounds, and I have many people to thank for helping me make my idea a reality. To begin with, I am grateful for the many research scientists who have conducted and continue to conduct important research expanding our knowledge about social media and its impact on our mental health—research that has informed this book.

Next, to Dr. Salman Akhtar I express my sincere gratitude for the time and knowledge he generously gave me and for connecting me to my publisher, Rowman & Littlefield. I also thank the Psychoanalytic Center of Philadelphia and all its members for their outstanding educational programs and for inspiring my continued passion for growing and learning.

My gratitude also extends to the team at *Main Line Today*: Hobart Rowland, editor-in-chief, and Lisa Dukart, senior editor, supported my writing and allowed me to be "the resident psychologist" for the Philadelphia area community. Without their support of my blog *Thinking*

Forward, I would have had neither the experience nor the courage to write this book.

I also sincerely appreciate my fantastic tribe—Allison, Laurie, Andrea, Amy, Heather, Jennie, Ellen, Kathy, Beth, and Gloria. Thank you for your friendship, encouragement, support, and willingness to read chapter drafts and, without judgments, to hear me out whenever I was feeling overwhelmed. To my best friend, Paulette, thank you for your pep talks and for showing me all the cool places in New York City to write—and for keeping me company too!

Words cannot express my gratitude and deep appreciation for my writing coach, Jennifer Divina, for her professional advice, unending patience, and assistance in polishing this manuscript. I also thank my editor at Rowman & Littlefield, Suzanne Staszak-Silva, for the constructive feedback and invaluable guidance she gave me while I was writing this book.

Special thanks go to Dr. Ruth Garfield, for being an incredible teacher about all things related to life. I thank my mom, Edith, for listening to me read chapters aloud to her. And, finally, I thank my husband, Larry, and our daughters, Sarah and Hope, for being my biggest supporters, my inspiration, my most important accomplishments, and my greatest joys in life.

INTRODUCTION

If your social media and digital habits have reached the point where you've lost control over your time, your attention span, or your ability to follow through with simple tasks or day-to-day responsibilities, if your relationships and your mental health are suffering, take heart—you're not alone!

We've all been there, spending hours and hours scanning Facebook, Instagram, Snapchat, or Twitter, poring over friends' and family's posts detailing their holiday season, their vacations, or their momentous occasions, which leaves us with feelings of depression, envy, unflattering comparison, and shame that bubble up inside us. Now, even more importantly, it's important to ask yourself these questions: "What was I expecting when I logged on, posted that picture, made that comment, tweeted that thought, or sent that text?"

What you might be surprised to learn, however, is that passively consuming social media and other forms of technology, *even when we're feeling pretty good about ourselves*, can result in our feeling way more sad, anxious, grumpy, annoyed, and irritable than we did moments before we logged on![1] The truth is that obsessively checking social media, e-mails, texts, and other virtual sites robs us of valuable time that could be used for our personal development and deepening our real-life relationships or forming new ones.

More and more, people come to my therapeutic practice and say,

"I'm constantly checking my phone and looking at social media to
the point where I'm anxious when I don't check and log in and
anxious when I do. I can't win either way!"

"My best friend posted pictures of her new baby, and here we are,
still trying to have a child after five years! I know I shouldn't go
on social media and look at other people's pictures of their new
babies, but I can't stop myself."

"I can't get anything done because I can't stop checking my phone!"

"When I look at social media, all I think is, *What's wrong with me?*"

"I haven't spoken to my mom in two years, and seeing her on social
media ruins my mood and whole day."

"I feel like my husband of fifteen years is a stranger. We can barely
get through a conversation for more than five minutes without
my yelling at him for being glued to his phone. This makes me so
sad. We never sit down and have a conversation, face-to-face,
with eye contact, and all."

For many of us, social media can feel like an unpredictable roller-
coaster ride. Our mood can swing from elated after getting a slew of
likes on a post, to worthless in response to being criticized in a comments thread. Depression and rejection can strike after you realize you
weren't invited to that get together you knew nothing about until logging on and seeing a picture of all your friends together, minus you.
Distant, repressed memories from long ago can surface and get jolted
into consciousness, causing an emotional meltdown you weren't expecting or ready to confront.

There's no doubt that social media has replaced traditional ways of
communicating and meeting other people to such a degree that it has
altered our experiences of play, connecting, exploration, dating, and
meeting new friends. As human beings, our social relationships are
crucial to our survival, emotional regulation, and overall mental health.
Studies have consistently demonstrated that having a positive support
network decreases the risk for depression, anxiety, and addiction. Our
relationships are also important in that they help us develop our understanding of who we are, our likes and dislikes, our passions, and our
interests. They help us form our identity, help others form their own
identities, aid in our understanding of the world we live in, and create
meaning and purpose in our lives.

Let me be clear: social media isn't and can't ever be a substitute for our real-life relationships, real-life conversations, and real-life experiences. Living a virtual life isn't equal to living an actual life. Yet for so many, social-media relationships and technology experiences outnumber real experiences. Psychologists believe that our social-media habits change our behaviors, attitudes, and personalities just as much as our real-life habits do.[2] For example, seeing a particular social-media post on any given day can have just as much influence over our decisions, thoughts, or outlook about a particular news story, idea, or goal as a real-life interaction can. That's a lot of influence and power!

Think about this fact: the average American spends more than ten hours a day glued to their screens. A recent study by the Pew Research Center found that eight in ten Americans have a Facebook profile, 32 percent have an Instagram account, and 24 percent have a Twitter account. It is predicted that by 2021, the number of social-media users worldwide will be over four billion.[3] Research shows we're spending an average of two hours every day sharing, liking, tweeting, and updating on these platforms. That breaks down to around half a million tweets and Snapchat photos shared every minute.

Every day, patients share with me the bad feelings they experience from their social-media interactions. These bad feelings often linger, affecting their offline lives and worsening any mental-health or relationship issues they're already contending with. People log on for all sorts of reasons: They might feel bored, unfocused, curious, lonely, depressed, or anxious and hope logging on will give them answers to their questions or lift their spirits by cultivating feelings of connection. After all, isn't being "social" supposed to be good for our mental health? Yet our feelings and our relationships, both in real life and in the virtual realm, aren't so simple or so black and white.

But it's not all bad news! Striking a healthy balance between the virtual life and actual life is really possible and can even lead to a more meaningful and enriched real-life existence. As you read through *Logged In and Stressed-Out*, you will learn about targeted actions and behaviors you can apply to your everyday life in order to gain better control over unhealthy social-media habits. But what is perhaps even more helpful and significant is that by reading this book, you'll be able to dig deeper into yourself in order to understand the whys underneath your self-destructive social-media habits. As with all self-destructive behaviors, whether they have to do with social media, addictions, or relationships, only when we have a true understanding of what we're trying to accomplish can we make effective, real, and lasting change.

For the past eighteen-plus years I've been in private practice, working together with people to help them live lives with intention, purpose, meaning, and joy! As the great psychoanalyst Sigmund Freud once said, "Love and work . . . work and love. What else is there, really?"[4] Certainly the ways in which we decide to spend our time and with whom—whether it be spending hours logged onto social media or having a relationship in our virtual or actual life—will have a great impact on our emotional health, outlook, and quality of life.

As you read through each chapter of *Logged In and Stressed-Out* you will learn

- How to deepen virtual relationships and boost IRL relationships
- How our attachment style impacts our "attachment" to devices, technology, and social media
- How to turn negative feelings resulting from social-media use into opportunities for emotional growth and personal development
- Why and how social media and technology can exacerbate an existing mental-health issue
- How to cope with loss and breakups in the digital age
- How to minimize virtual conflicts, virtual misunderstandings, and after-posting regrets
- How to cultivate mindfulness in the digital age and
- How to strike the perfect balance between the virtual life and actual life and why finding balance is important for our well-being and relationships.

So let's get started!

Please note—the case vignettes you will be reading throughout this book are composites and not based on an actual person. Any details resembling a particular person are completely coincidental.

I

BUILDING RELATIONSHIPS IN THE DIGITAL AGE

How bold one gets when one is sure of being loved!

—Sigmund Freud[1]

There's no doubt that our relationships are front and center in determining our emotional and physical health. We thrive when we have close, long-term relationships and mutually supportive friendships. Having positive relationships lengthens our life span, boosts our immunity, and improves our emotional well-being.[2] Roman philosopher Seneca once said, "One of the most beautiful qualities of true friendship is to understand and to be understood."[3]

Since the advent of the iPhone, social media, and apps, however, the ways in which we go about nurturing and tending to our important relationships have forever changed. Whereas only a few years ago we communicated personal news via phone conversations or actual in-person encounters, today most people use computer-mediated communication (CMC), like texting, instant messaging, Snapchat, Instagram, Twitter, Facebook, or e-mail to catch up with friends and family. Think about the last time you shared something about yourself with your friends. It is likely you sent a text, posted a status update on Facebook, uploaded pictures on Instagram, or sent a Snapchat. Many psychologists—myself included—question whether or not today's whirlwind of connectedness through technology and devices has actually left us feeling more disconnected and emotionally empty than ever.

In my practice, all too often I hear people say,

"I have over five hundred friends and followers, but I still feel so
   alone."
"I never learned how to have a conversation in person or over the
   phone."
"I don't know what it's like to go out on an actual date!"
"I'm afraid to talk to people IRL."

It is likely that you, like many people, have had similar thoughts and
have wondered what you can do about them. In this chapter, we'll take
a closer look at these feelings and how changing our interactions with
technology and social media can improve our relationships. You'll meet
Mike, a millennial struggling with forming personal connections that go
beyond just hooking up, and Jessie, who's having a virtual emotional
affair with someone she hasn't seen or spoken with on the phone in over
three years. But first, let's examine why our relationships are so important in the first place.

UNPACKING RELATIONSHIPS

Why is socializing in person so important? To understand the answer,
we need to look to some of the foundational theories of psychology. Our
drive to form relationships has motivations well beyond deriving the
obvious psychologically beneficial feelings of belonging, connection, affiliation, and understanding: forming relationships is also crucial to our
survival as a species. Humans evolved into social beings out of necessity.
Dependence on and cooperation with each other enhanced our ability
to survive the harsh environmental circumstances we faced centuries
ago.[4] Although certain threats to our survival have lessened in today's
world, one thing is for sure: humans still have an innate need and drive
to affiliate with one another. In fact, the lack of such connections in
one's life can produce problematic feelings of loneliness.

Famous psychologist Abraham Maslow developed a now-well-
known theory to illuminate our innate need for belonging and love. This
theory, known as Maslow's hierarchy of needs, breaks down human
needs and human motivation into five sequential levels.[5] Each level
builds upon the previous level, and our needs are fulfilled in a specific

order. Only when a prior need is satisfied can one begin working on achieving the next level. Based on Maslow's theory, our first and most important need is our physiological care—including proper nutrition, water, and sleep. Our second-level need is safety—which encompasses shelter, employment, and health. Our third-level need is love and belonging—reflecting our need to have friends and family. This level of need is what Maslow refers to as our *social needs*. The fourth-level need is esteem—including confidence, self-esteem, and a sense of achievement. Finally, our last need is for self-actualization. Achieving self-actualization is thought to be crucial to our existence. Self-actualization is a big and complex concept, but it's basically a need for morality, creativity, and acceptance. Self-actualization reflects our full potential. It is important to note that belonging ranks third on Maslow's hierarchy, after physiological and safety needs have been met, but before an individual can pursue esteem and self-actualization.

Erik Erikson is a well-known psychoanalyst who examined the importance our relationships have on our emotional well-being. Unlike other psychologists and psychoanalysts of his day—most notably Sigmund Freud—Erikson developed theories that took into account the impact culture, society, and family have on personality development and mental health. In short, Erikson's theory is comprised of eight developmental crises, beginning at birth and ending at death. He believed that successfully working through a specific crisis during specific points in our development is crucial for developing a healthy and adaptive personality.[6] Erikson called the developmental crisis most relevant to cultivating healthy relationships in the digital age *love—intimacy versus isolation*. This crisis is the first encountered in adult development, occurring during our young adulthood, beginning at around age eighteen and lasting until forty years old. Developing the skills for establishing and forming lifelong intimate relationships—such as friendships, romantic partners, and starting a family—is the key challenge at this stage. The capacity to actually feel love and intimacy is necessary for feeling safe and cared for as well as for cultivating a deep sense of commitment to important relationships in our lives. Based on Erikson's theory, if someone is not able to work through this developmental crisis, most likely they will have difficulty forming and maintaining meaningful and nurturing relationships.

A whole body of psychology and method of psychotherapy focuses on the quality of an individual's relationships: *relational psychology*, as it's called, suggests that the way people relate to others and situations in their adult lives is shaped by family experiences during infancy and childhood.[7] For example, a person who had experienced neglect or abuse in infancy would as an adult expect similar behavior from others who remind them of the neglectful or abusive parent from their past.

MEET MIKE

When I spoke with Mike by phone before he came to see me for his first therapy appointment, he told me he was feeling great about the progress he was making in his career. He had just graduated from a top university and landed his first job, and he was living on his own. But, as he said with restraint, in an attempt to cover his disappointment, "I'm not having much success in the relationship department. I've never been in a real relationship, and I can't figure out why!"

During Mike's first sessions, he would often stress, "I've worked so hard my whole life! I got into my dream college, and I have a great job now, but I'm feeling more lonely than ever. And when I go on Facebook, Instagram, and Snapchat and see pictures of my friends with their boyfriends and girlfriends, I can't help asking myself, why can't I be in a relationship too?" Mike continued, "I've even tried Tinder and Bumble with zero luck."

I've heard stories like Mike's many times. Lots of the young adults I see in my practice say the same thing: "I've worked hard my whole life, got into a great college, landed a good job, but my relationships are not clicking." So what's keeping Mike and others like him from making meaningful personal connections?

It is the *work* that's involved in building emotional ties that is a mystery to them, and that work is where Mike and I focused our energy. In our sessions, I observed that Mike often used texting as his main means of communicating with someone he was interested in, and he rarely called anyone, even his friends. It hadn't occurred to him that the ways he was communicating with others might be as important as what he was communicating.

The invention of apps, social media, and various dating platforms has significantly altered the ways in which people socialize, meet, date, and develop the relationships that later turn into long-term committed ones. More and more I hear from the single adults I treat just how difficult it is to forge relationships in the digital age. At these times, I find myself reflecting back on how people met before the Internet and complementary technologies evolved. For me, that time was from around the mid-1980s to the mid-1990s. In those days, people connected through friendships, in classes, or at social gatherings like parties or religious or community events. Now, in the digital age, it's more common for people to meet online or through a dating app than in person.

Eventually, Mike uncovered the mysteries of how to build relationships without only relying on technology. Although this was challenging for him, through overcoming his stress about in-person encounters and talking on the phone, (after all, he didn't have much experience), Mike went on to form relationships that nurtured him, and he eventually started dating someone he really liked. Most importantly, Mike learned how to talk to people and how to be in the presence of others without a screen by developing the ability to have emotionally intimate relationships. Let's now focus on the steps necessary for developing emotional intimacy so you too can have satisfying relationships in the digital age.

EMOTIONAL INTIMACY IS KEY TO BUILDING GENUINE RELATIONSHIPS

How emotionally intimate are your relationships? Measure yourself using the Emotional Intimacy Scale, developed by researchers Vaughn G. Sinclair and Sharon W. Dowdy.[8]

Write down a list of all the people you consider to be most important to you. Next to each name, jot down how much (rarely, a little bit, a moderate amount, quite a bit, a great deal of the time) you feel the following regarding each one. Be honest, and try not to judge yourself or your loved ones. There is always room for growth. There will be suggestions throughout this book for how to deepen your relationships with others and, most importantly, yourself!

- They accept me for who I am.

- I can openly share my deepest thoughts and feelings with them.
- They care deeply for me.
- They are willing to help me in any way.
- I feel understood and affirmed by them.

Based on decades of my clinical experience and training, it's not just having people in our lives that supports our emotional and physical health. In fact, many people who are already in relationships enter therapy because they want to work on improving their relationships. As Maslow realized, our need for belonging also includes our need to give and receive love. A major component for being loved and being able to love is having the ability to cultivate *emotional intimacy*.

The word "intimacy" is derived from the Latin *intimus*, meaning "inner" or "innermost." To be intimate with another is to have access to, and to comprehend, that person's innermost character. Philosopher Gabriel Marcel poetically defined intimacy: "Even if I cannot see you, if I cannot touch you, I feel that you are with me."[9]

There's no question that emotionally intimate relationships deepens our feelings of belonging, helps us regulate our emotions, and add richness, purpose, meaning, direction, and focus to our lives. In fact, nothing else in life can really compare to the power and meaning our relationships have over our experience of life. We've all heard the expression that money can't buy happiness. In large part this is because most things in life outside of our relationships can't fill us up or gratify us as much as can the people with whom we share our lives.

Emotional intimacy is a complex concept; after all it's the foundation for all of our close relationships. Close emotional intimacy in a relationship is felt when we feel so safe and secure that we are able to share our true feelings, be our authentic selves, and reveal our vulnerabilities to another person who, in response to us, provides us with genuine understanding, affirmation, and care. Emotionally intimate relationships are not just one-sided; they are reciprocal. So interdependency—the delicate balance between dependency and independence—is the hallmark of emotionally intimate relationships. Interdependency affords us the ability to be autonomous while at the same time dependent.

Self-disclosure is necessary for cultivating emotional intimacy. Self-disclosure is the actual act of sharing with another person our innermost being—or essence. This means revealing our fears, self-doubts, and weakness as well as our strengths and competencies. And the more often we share our intimate feelings with others, the more intimate our relationships will be. Although this might seem obvious to some, for others revealing intimate parts of themselves feels counterintuitive and even foreign, because they fear that doing so will make them appear weak. It's tough to open up to others when we're afraid of what people might see or think. And if we weren't raised in an environment that modeled, supported, and encouraged honest communications, we simply don't know *how to* share our feelings and fears.

Many psychologists believe that the kind of intimacy that emerges between people in online interactions is different than intimacy created offline and affirm that digital interaction redefines intimacy and reduces it to easy connections. "When technology engineers intimacy," says one expert in social studies and technology, "relationships can be reduced to mere connections. And then, easy connection becomes redefined as intimacy."[10] On the other hand, we may develop intimate relationships with people we meet online or with whom we usually interact through social media due to the easy accessibility we have to them via digital communication. And then there are other researchers who believe that whenever intimacy is made public it ceases to be intimacy—that it loses its status when it is advertised.[11]

Although there's a lot of debate regarding whether or not truly emotionally intimate relationships exist in the virtual world, one thing is for sure: we learn how to have emotionally intimate relationships from our early relationships, most notably our relationship with our early caregivers and our family of origin. These early relationships carry great importance, because they set the tone and foundation for all our future ones, including our digital relationships. Not everyone is fortunate enough to have had healthy early relationships. As infants, toddlers, young children, and adolescents, we all looked to our parents to meet our attachment and relational needs and to help us grow and mature emotionally so we could become independent enough to care and nurture the next generation.

It's okay if most or even if all of your relationships are not as emotionally intimate as you would like them to be. Cultivating emotional intimacy is possible, and it's never too late to learn.

SKILL-BUILDING STRATEGY

Having intimate relationships takes work. With practice, patience, and commitment you can learn to develop intimate relationships and deepen already-established ones. Below are three tips you can use right away to deepen your relationships.

- Maintain eye contact during conversations. This communicates interest, openness, and willingness to hear what the other person has to say.
- Show interest in other people. Really listen to other people's feelings, opinions, and life experiences. Make sure to put your devices away too!
- Be authentic. We cannot have emotionally intimate relationships if we're being fake or insincere.
- Be truthful. None of us likes being lied to, especially from those we are close to. For many, being truthful is hard. But it's important to work on taking responsibility for our actions. Telling the truth is the basis for all trustworthy and secure relationships, which in turn are the hallmarks of emotionally intimate relationships.

I believe that it is important not only to understand which factors create good relationships and improve our existing relationships but also to learn about the signs and signals that are hallmarks of bad relationships. We suffer when we have relationships that are turbulent and toxic. Negative relationships not only wear us down emotionally and physically but also can stop us from reaching what Maslow refers to as the "self-actualized life," living a life to our fullest potential.

For example, some types of emotional abuse, unlike physical and sexual abuse, can be much harder to pinpoint and recognize. This is because emotional abuse often is inconsistent and happens in multiple forms. But at its core, all forms of emotional abuse play into our human fears of rejection, abandonment, unworthiness, shame, and unlovability.

It is important to note that people who were emotionally abused as children are at greater risk of becoming victims of emotional abuse as adults. If you or a loved one is a victim of emotional abuse, it is important to seek help from a professional. There is hope for a better future.

Beware of the following common forms of emotional abuse.

- Stonewalling. Not all emotional abuse is verbal or involves shouting or criticism. *Stonewalling* is cutting off all communication by giving someone the silent treatment until they do what you want them to do. Refusing to see the other person's perspective by minimization or disengagement is another form of stonewalling.
- Emotional withholding. When a person withholds love and affection in order to communicate anger, they are being *emotionally withholding*, which creates a great deal of anxiety in the victim, as it plays into our human fears of rejection, abandonment, and unworthiness of love.
- Twisting. When the victim confronts the abuser, the abuser deflects attention from themselves by *twisting* facts around in order to place blame or responsibility onto the victim. They then demand an apology to avoid taking responsibility for their actions. Bouts of intense rage and fury without obvious or rational cause can create a great amount of fear and uncertainty in the victim. Intense rage episodes are shocking and startling for everyone. The aim of twisting is to force the victim into silence and compliance.
- Trivializing accomplishments. Emotional abusers need to feel dominant and superior in order to cope with their deep-seated feelings of inferiority, shame, and envy. Tactics of *trivializing others' accomplishments* include mockery, belittling goals, ignoring accomplishments, and finding ways to sabotage another from achieving their own accomplishments. [12]

Next, let's consider the problem of making fake connections in the digital age.

MEET JESSIE

For the past two and a half years, Jessie has been carrying on a secret virtual relationship via texting with Steve, a fellow nurse she met at her last job. Jessie and her husband have since moved to another state, and Jessie has not seen Steve for several years.

"I know this sounds messed up," Jessie exclaimed in session one day, "but I feel Steve really knows me—in fact even more so than my own husband. Our virtual relationship feels really intimate."

Jessie and her husband, Kevin, have been married for a little over five years, and they have a two-year-old son. "I haven't actually seen Steve since I stopped working, and that was three years ago, so it's confusing how I can feel so close to him. I know it's wrong, and I know that if I continue this 'virtual affair' it will ruin my marriage. I just don't know how to stop it!"

A striking aspect of Jessie's relationship with Steve is that it all takes place virtually—only by text. Yet this reality doesn't seem to affect Jessie's feelings for Steve. The fact that Jessie hasn't actually been in Steve's physical presence hasn't affected her emotional connection with or longing for Steve. Our digital experiences, interactions, and relationships can cultivate a unique feeling of what psychologists refer to as *social presence*. Social presence is a feeling—one that is not always accurate or genuine—of emotional closeness and intimacy with another individual from afar.[13] The factors that contribute to social presence have a lot to do with the immediacy that technology affords us. But there is another side to the social-presence phenomenon that does not engender emotional intimacy: since the digital age allows us to live an edited life, we can choose when to view and reply to messages at our own convenience or simply whenever we feel like it. In addition, the experience of social presence—that is, feeling emotionally attuned and emotionally intimate to a person through texting—doesn't mean our experience is "real." After all, how do we really know anything when we can't see, feel, and touch another?

Furthermore, *computer-mediated communication*, like texting, WhatsApp, or iMessage, can inhibit our ability to develop emotional intimacy, because CMC, as it is known, is what scholars refer to as *asynchronous communication*.[14] Asynchronous communications don't happen in real time. In the digital age, we get to choose when to view and when to reply to messages. It's no surprise to learn that asynchronous communications can leave us feeling emotionally distant and empty. This is especially so when relationships—like Jessie's relationship with Steve—are made up of mainly computer-mediated communication that's inconsistent and ambiguous, leading us to question whether or not there's anyone on the other end of our device.

BACK TO JESSIE

Jessie was clear about the fact that she didn't want to end her marriage with Kevin. And Jessie was willing to examine the experiences from her past that were possibly influencing her current actions. For example, Jessie's father had multiple affairs when she was growing up. And she was willing to examine the factors from her present life as well that were also contributing to her carrying on an emotional affair with Steve, like the stressors of being a stay-at-home wife and mother and the demands of parenting their young son.

Over time, Jessie came to understand that her virtual affair was pushing her to lead a "fake" life, in that her intense feelings toward Steve were to a degree a creation of own projections and internal fantasies.

One day in session, Jessie even asked herself, "How am I to be certain that it was in fact Steve who was actually texting me and not some friend of his?" Jessie was asking herself good questions. But they were the kinds of questions we rarely ask ourselves when we feel a genuinely intimate bond with another person. Over time, Jessie learned to be more open and authentic with Kevin and to be able to express her true needs, feelings, and desires. One way she did this was by simply taking a break from social media and technology altogether, allowing herself the space and time she needed to think things through.

TAKE TIME OFF TECHNOLOGY TO BOOST YOUR RELATIONSHIPS IN REAL LIFE

Because of our connectivity, we spend an average of two hours every day sharing, liking, tweeting, and updating on social-media platforms. Unsurprisingly, spending hours looking at our screens increases our risk for depression, anxiety, and loneliness and erodes our ability to have satisfying relationships in real life—not to mention the precious time we rob ourselves of that could be used for personal and emotional development.

SKILL-BUILDING STRATEGIES

Consider these five ways to take some time off social media and technology.

- Catch up in person. Cultivating emotional intimacy is necessary for close relationships. It's important to feel, see, and experience emotions in person, not just through a digital filter.
- Do something creative. Try painting, drawing, writing, or knitting. Creative activities improve our mood and reduce anxiety.
- Connect with nature. Go for a walk, hike, or run. Sitting in front of a screen for hours is not only bad for our health; it's also bad for our emotional well-being.
- Commit to practicing mindfulness meditation at least once a day. Mindfulness is about being present in the small moments.

INCREASING EMOTIONAL INTIMACY IN THE DIGITAL AGE

Forming and maintaining relationships in the digital age is more complicated than it has ever been before for humans. We are faced with the task of learning how to have relationships in real time while simultaneously figuring out how to form healthy and satisfying virtual ones. In fact, there's good reason to believe that we treat our CMCs—and the phones that contain them—like we treat our relationships in general based on current studies examining our relationship to our devices through the lens of attachment theory.[15] And guess what? We treat our phones much the same way.

It's not all bad news, though. At a recent dinner party I attended, I had the great pleasure of talking with a friend's mother about how she was able to visit Paris virtually with her granddaughter. She proceeded to tell me that she had never been to Paris and due to physical limitations would never be able to in her lifetime. However, her granddaughter would often FaceTime her from Paris and "bring her grandmother along with her," as she saw the wonderful sights in real life. My friend's mother exclaimed, "Even though I've never been to Paris or visited the Eiffel Tower, in some real ways I feel I have. When my granddaughter would FaceTime me, it felt like I was really there with her!"

Another story comes to mind that illustrates the power of technology deepening our emotional intimacy with others. It happened while I was away with extended family. At that time, our cousin's two sons were literally across the country, visiting our other family members and having a vacation of their own. I was intrigued to see how my cousin stayed closely connected to her sons while they were miles apart, each engaged in exciting activities with our other family members. Her sons used FaceTime to stay connected, and they enriched their text communications by sending pictures and video. Technology was connecting them in ways that weren't possible in the predigital era.

Following are a few strategies you can start using right away to deepen your relationships—both virtual and real-life.

RECOMMENDATIONS

1. Keep a journal of your social-media habits. Record how many times per day you log on to social media and the amount of time you spend on these sites. Take note of things like the time of day you are most likely to log on and how you feel before and after you log on. For many of us, logging on to social media is a reflexive behavior. Getting honest with yourself about how often you interact with social media on a daily basis is a big step toward cultivating self-awareness.

2. Commit to making your closest relationships emotionally intimate. Emotional intimacy is built up over time. Practice being open and vulnerable in the presence of a person you trust, like a best friend, partner, or family member.

3. Increase your rich-media communications. An example would be communicating by FaceTime, Skype, or video conferencing. Being able to talk in real time and being able to see the person's body language and hearing their vocal tone and inflictions are important components for developing genuine emotional attunement and emotional intimacy.

4. Make digital-sharing multimedia. For example, include pictures and videos in your CMCs to increase feelings of genuine social presence and emotional intimacy by simply allowing others to see you.

2

SCREEN ATTACHMENTS

Life is best organized as a series of daring adventures from a secure base.

—John Bowlby[1]

Is social media making you more anxious? Are your virtual relationships stressing you out? Have you ever had social-media regret because you overshared in a post? Do you go into panic mode when you don't have your phone? If you've answered yes to one or more of these questions, your problems with social media might be related to your attachment style.

Think about this: a recent study by a global technology protection company found that, on average, Americans check their phones fifty-two times per day.[2] With an estimated population of 270 million Americans, that means we're viewing our smartphones approximately fourteen billion times daily. Another study found that Americans check their iPhones once every twelve minutes. That's twenty-eight times more per day than the findings from the first study mentioned.

There's no denying it: we are attached to our devices. I couldn't imagine life without technology and my smartphone. Like the 270 million Americans, I check my smartphone more than I want to admit! I use it for storing pictures, my contacts, and a calendar, tracking my fitness and activity, reading my e-mails and texts, catching up on the news, making restaurant reservations, surfing the Web while on the go, and of course checking in on my social-media accounts. Although there might be some debate regarding the exact number of times on average we engage with our devices, one thing is for sure: we spend much of our existence glued to our screens.

Recently a number of studies have been conducted examining the relationship between our attachment style—the characteristic ways in which we learn to relate to others from our earliest relationships—and our social-media habits. Not surprisingly, findings from these studies suggest that our attachment styles do, in fact, impact online social interactions in much the same way that they do offline. Furthermore, these studies also indicated that certain attachment styles, when compared to others, are more prone to experiencing negative social and emotional consequences from use of social media.[3]

In an environment where we can initiate and manage online and offline social connections, social media not only serves as a means of entertainment and socializing, but it also serves attachment functions. In this chapter, you'll learn about the origins of attachment theory, the three main categories of attachment (secure, anxious, and avoidant), the basic behavioral characteristics of each attachment style, and how specific attachment styles affect well-being and relationships, both online and offline.

A BRIEF PRIMER ON ATTACHMENT

What exactly does *attachment* mean? Why and how humans form attachments has always been of great interest to psychologists and scholars in the social sciences. John Bowlby, a British psychoanalyst, is the pioneer of the evolutionary theory of attachment. His theory purports that all humans have an innate, biological predisposition to form attachments and that our drive to build attachments is instinctual and crucial to our survival. Simply put, our lives depend on our attachments.

Furthermore, the quality of our early relationships with our caregivers is crucial. This relationship sets the stage for the health and success of our future relationships. One reason our early relationships are as influential as they are in the kinds of attachments we'll form over our life span is because our early relationships determine what's known as our *internal working model* of the world. We all have an internal working model. It guides our thoughts, behaviors, moods, and expectations about how others will behave and react toward us; essentially, our internal working models set the rules and expectations for us regarding how we believe a relationships works. "I generally believe people are trust worthy" or "People will take advantage of me and disappoint me" or "I can rely on my friends and family to help me" are all examples of internal working models.[4] In a nutshell, attachment theory focuses on how people connect with others. One can think of attachment style as being analogous to a relationship style or relationship pattern.

THE THREE MAIN ATTACHMENT STYLES

Psychologist Mary Ainsworth is best known for expanding upon Bowlby's evolutionary theory of attachment through her research examining young children's separations and reunions with their mothers. Based on numerous observations of mother-child dyads, Ainsworth came up with three general styles of human attachment:

1. Secure attachment. If you were lucky enough to have early caregivers who were consistently available, emotionally attuned, empathetic, and responsive to your needs, most likely you'll fall into this category. People with secure attachment styles tend to exhibit confidence, healthy self-esteem, and an ability to regulate emotions and are more likely to have and enjoy healthy reciprocal relationships.

2. Anxious attachment. Anxious attachments are likely to be formed if your early caregivers were inconsistent with their ability to be responsive, empathic, and emotionally attuned. As adults, anxiously attached individuals tend to doubt their self-worth, show higher degrees of ambivalence, fear rejection, seek reassurance and approval, and long for constant closeness. When the anxiously attached are emotionally distressed, the urge to connect with others is heightened, and efforts made to connect often bring about negative emotional consequences.

3. Avoidant attachment. This style of attachment is thought to be a consequence of an early caregiver's general lack of availability and responsiveness. As adults, avoidantly attached individuals can be excessively self-reliant and mistrustful and might avoid intimacy. People in this group tend to use attachment-deactivating

strategies—for example, never showing an outward desire for closeness or affection in most of their relationships.[5]

MEET KAYLA, AN ANXIOUSLY ATTACHED SOCIAL-MEDIA USER

Kayla, a petite and strikingly attractive twenty-five-year-old and second-year law student, cried out in session, "I'm so attached to my computer that I can't sleep without it!" Kayla initially came to me for treatment for help to improve her friendships and her romantic and professional relationships. Ever since Kayla could remember, she'd struggled to form meaningful and lasting attachments.

"Making friends is not as much a problem for me as is developing deeper relationships that I feel good about and safe in," she told me. "I know I can get too clingy and too needy for attention, emotional support, and reassurance. I'm always worried about what my friends think of me."

Recently, Kayla expressed feeling upset with her virtual relationships as well. A few people unfriended her on Facebook, some stopped following her Instagram account, and others ignored her Snapchats. Kayla also complained about not getting as much attention or reaction from her posts, status updates, selfies, and pictures as she had in the past.

Kayla noticed a pattern of posting in which she would rev up her social-media activity when she felt emotional distress—for example, if she had a bad day at school or an argument with her mother. During times of emotional upheaval, Kayla would spend hours upon hours glued to her computer, logged on to social media, engrossed in a "frantic frenzy" of posting. She'd meticulously craft "perfect posts," revealing her feelings, thoughts, and whereabouts, with the goal of engaging in any kind of interaction to combat her anxiety and bad moods.

> During these moments, I go on posting binges, hoping my virtual friends will tell me what to do, how to handle my situation, and reassure me that everything will be okay. When my friends do respond with comments, likes, or emoji, I feel better, but only for a little while. At other times, it makes me feel more anxious and depressed, because I end up confused and feeling regretful about my social-media actions, reputation, and relationships on top of all the

other issues I already struggle with in my real life! I realize I need to learn why I act this way and how to stop going on social media looking for comfort. Most importantly, I need to learn how I can help myself when I'm upset in my *actual* life.

The Pew Research Center began tracking Americans' social-media consumption in 2005. At that time, only 5 percent of Americans used at least one social-media platform.[6] Today, over 75 percent of Americans have at least one social-media account. And many people, like Kayla, turn to their virtual friends and followers on social-media sites like Facebook, Instagram, Snapchat, and LinkedIn as a way to fulfill their attachment needs.

As I got to know Kayla better, it became clear that her struggles with relationships both online and offline were, in part, due to her anxious attachment style. Kayla was using her social-media friends as a "base" to go to when she needed emotional warmth and reassurance. But since Kayla's way of relating to others was characteristic of an anxious attachment, her attempts to connect to her friends often made her feel more anxious instead of secure. We tend to treat others the same ways we were treated; history repeats itself through our attachments. So, securely attached parents are likely to raise securely attached kids. Anxiously and avoidantly attached parents are likely to raise anxiously attached kids who later become anxiously or avoidantly attached adults. Kayla's behaviors, though typical for an anxiously attached adult, were confusing to her friends, causing them to pull away from her at times.

BACK TO KAYLA

"Sometimes my parents were emotionally available, and at other times they completely ignored me," Kayla told me in session.

> So as a kid, I often felt confused and anxious! I never knew what to expect from my parents. But I learned early that in order to get their attention I had to be clingy or in a state of desperation. Especially with my mom: she was anxious and self-absorbed when I was growing up, and unfortunately she still is today. I never felt my parents really had my back. This made me not trust them and others in my life.

I now realize how having emotionally unreliable parents affected my ability to trust others, damaged my self-esteem, my self-concept, and my ability to cope, especially with my anxiety, in healthier ways. It's also why I'm constantly seeking reassurance from my friends. I hope I can be the mom I always wanted when I eventually have my kids.

ANXIOUS ATTACHMENT, SOCIAL MEDIA, AND WELL-BEING

Studies examining the relationship between attachment styles and social media indicate that those with anxious attachments, like Kayla, misuse social media, using it as a means for meeting their attachment needs. Anxiously attached social-media users often overshare to fulfill the need for belonging and reassurance. They are also overly concerned with their online impressions, spending an excessive amount of time crafting comments and photoshopping uploaded pictures to their social-networking sites to fulfill their need for validation.[7]

Another consequence related to anxiously attached social media users is a reported increase in anxiety after being online. The use of social-networking sites can trigger a "cycle of anxiety" for anxiously attached individuals by simultaneously acting as a trigger for relationship anxiety and a coping tool for anxiety reduction when emotionally distressed. This cycle, in part, is because insecurely attached people are preoccupied with how others perceive them. They look to others for reassurance and emotional support and are more likely to struggle with low self-esteem. Kayla was able to identify this pattern of behavior playing out in her relationships.

A significant goal of Kayla's treatment was to learn how to develop secure relationships. Fortunately, a person's style of attachment can be revised through new experiences, interacting with a partner who has a history of being securely attached, and making sense of one's past through psychotherapy.

First, Kayla and I worked hard to establish a therapeutic relationship that allowed her to feel secure enough to open up and take emotional risks in sessions. Second, Kayla and I examined both her present and past relationships in which she felt somewhat secure. Kayla had a loving relationship with a grandmother who had died when she was twelve years old. Presently, she has an aunt she has a good relationship with who acts as a stand-in for her mother at times in Kayla's life when she can benefit from a mother-like figure.

In sessions, Kayla spent a lot of time remembering and examining her more secure and healthier relationships. And for the first time, Kayla began forming new relationships that were more secure. She was now able to identify a model of secure attachment that guided her future relationships. Over time, Kayla learned how to manage her anxiety skillfully. She used less externalizing coping styles, like posting social-media broadcasts when feeling emotionally distressed. Kayla also began to use more personalized methods of computer-mediated communications, like Skype, FaceTime, and private and instant messaging. She found this type of CMC actually to deepen her virtual relationships. Multimedia communication allowed Kayla to maintain eye contact and hear the person's tone of voice she was interacting with, which reduced the chances for ambiguity, and which in turn greatly reduced Kayla's anxiety.

In Kayla's final session with me, she exclaimed, "I feel as though I'm getting to know my friends and myself on a deeper level! Having more stable and secure relationships makes me feel calmer in general. I no longer get overly anxious or freaked out when I don't get an immediate response or reaction from my friends."

For the first time in her life, Kayla has genuine, reciprocal interactions and relationships, both online and offline. "It feels good to no longer have to frantically attach myself to just anyone so I can stop feeling miserable. I'm learning to depend on myself more and even to enjoy time on my own. I'm also being selective about who I decide to spend my time with."

Kayla's self-esteem dramatically improved, along with her ability to validate her emotions, trust her decisions, and feel secure in her capabilities. Kayla was well on her way. She was building up her sense of self, and she was forming secure and positive relationships both online and off. If you fall into the anxiously or avoidantly attachment categories, don't despair. As I've said, attachment styles can be made to feel more secure through new experiences, new relationships, psychotherapy, and gaining an understanding of past relationships.

SELF-LOVE COMES FROM SECURE ATTACHMENT

Making lasting changes also means working on improving our most important relationship—the relationship we have with ourselves. As with most things psychological, a good place to start is working on cultivating self-love. Self-love is a natural by-product of secure attachments. Having self-love is not the same as being narcissistic or selfish. Instead, it means having positive regard for your own well-being and happiness. When we adopt an attitude of self-love, we have higher levels of self-esteem and we're less critical and harsh with ourselves when we make mistakes. We're able to celebrate our positive qualities and accept our negative ones. Also, a significant benefit to learning to love ourselves is that we are more likely to have fulfilling and healthy relationships.

SKILL-BUILDING STRATEGIES

Everyone, no matter their style of attachment, can benefit from practicing self-love. Below are a few strategies you can implement in your daily life to help you get started.

- Practice self-compassion. For many, it feels more natural to be compassionate toward friends and family than toward ourselves. Try eliminating critical and harsh self-talk. Imagining what you would say to a friend in the same situation should help you develop skills for positive self-talk.
- Enjoy time alone. Whether it's taking a walk in the park, going out for a nice meal, or seeing a great movie, learning to enjoy your own company and doing solo activities you find fulfilling is crucial for cultivating self-love.
- Make a list of all the characteristics you like about yourself. Too often we get caught up with only thinking about what it is we don't like about ourselves and what we wish we could change. For most of us, recognizing and appreciating our positive qualities takes effort and practice. Set aside time to read this list daily.

- Celebrate your accomplishments. No matter how big or small our successes or achievements are, it's important to feel worthy of celebrating them. Celebrating them reinforces our acknowledgment and integration of our positive qualities.
- Give yourself permission to ask for help. We all need support when life gets challenging and we feel overwhelmed. Most of life's challenges can't be tackled alone. Allowing ourselves to seek help from trusted friends or professionals reflects self-love.

MEET JOANNE

Joanne, in her mid-fifties and a stay-at-home mom, compulsively spent her days scrolling through her friends' social-media profiles on Facebook, Instagram, LinkedIn, Twitter, and Pinterest. She'd spend hours studying other people's status updates, check-ins, and pictures, only to find herself deep in a destructive rabbit hole of time lost in order to avoid thinking about how lonely, scared, and sad she always felt. Her oldest daughter was about to leave for college in just a few months. The few friends Joanne had, used social media to post pictures of their families and updates about their lives. On the one hand, social media seemed foolish to Joanne. "I can't understand why anyone would share their lives with the world!" Secretly, however, Joanne admitted she was very concerned about how others perceived her on social media.

On the rare occasion she did post anything, she'd carefully consider which pictures to post, making sure they showed her and her family at their very best. Joanne also secretly longed to have close relationships, but she didn't know how to be emotionally supportive to others, especially to her family. Joanne's inner critic—"I'm fine being alone" or "I don't need close friends"—stopped her from getting close to people, and her defensive style of relating to others was interfering with her having fuller and more joyful relationships. In a nutshell, Joanne was missing out on what makes life great—having close relationships with those we love.

THE SIGNIFICANCE OF THE PARENTAL MIRROR

For us to develop into healthy adults with ambitions, goals, and self-esteem, as young children we needed to receive a certain degree of positive attention from our parents or parent substitutes. One crucial way in which parents give their children positive attention is by mirroring. Parents mirror their young children when they validate them, confirm them, and take great pleasure in their unique sense of self and achievements. Mirroring is also an essential building block for developing secure attachments and healthy self-esteem, because the act of mirroring over time is what we need in order to develop a healthy degree of confidence and emotional stability and a cohesive identity. Parental mirroring is also vital for the development of healthy emotional regulation, empathy, and creativity.[8]

Sites like Facebook and Instagram provide us with an endless abundance of social comparison opportunities; we can access them at any time and any place. The absence of mirroring and validation in our early years, characteristic of anxiously and avoidantly attached childhoods, inhibits the cultivation of healthy self-esteem and the development of a cohesive sense of self and strong identity. It's unsurprising that many anxiously and avoidantly attached individuals also struggle with feeling empty and inadequate. As adults, anxiously and avoidantly attached individuals are more likely to rely on social comparisons as a means for reassurance and for finding answers to life's questions, like, "What should I do with my life?" "How should I behave?" "Whom should I marry?" "What kind of parent should I be?" "Where should I go for vacation?" "What should I be interested in doing?"

I will discuss the influence of social media on social comparisons in more detail in chapter 3.

HEALTHY SELF-ESTEEM AS A BY-PRODUCT OF SECURE ATTACHMENT

Have you ever wondered what self-esteem is? Have you ever thought you had low self-esteem? Have you ever wondered what you can do to raise your self-esteem?

Self-esteem is a psychological term that defines our general evaluation of our overall worth as an individual and is a natural by-product of secure attachments. These evaluations are based on our judgments about ourselves and the attitudes we have about ourselves—for example, our beliefs about our competency. *I am a worthy individual, and I have belief in my abilities,* or *I am not smart and not good at anything.* Self-esteem also encompasses the emotions we feel about ourselves—for example, feelings of pride and triumph or feelings of despair and shame. In a nutshell, self-esteem is the judgments we make and the emotions we feel about who we are, as well as our beliefs about how others perceive us. When our overarching self-evaluations are negative, we experience low self-esteem; we feel discouraged, undeserving, and unworthy. Conversely, we have high self-esteem when we have positive self-evaluations; we feel worthy, valued, and encouraged. Self-esteem also affects the way we behave and how we relate to others (i.e., compassionate and empathetic or defensive and judgmental).

In childhood, parents have the most influence on shaping self-esteem. The more positive early experiences we have, the higher the chance we will develop a secure attachment and, consequently, a healthy degree of self-confidence as children and adults. Numerous books and several studies have been conducted that show that parents who give their children unconditional love and respect raise children with high self-esteem. Conversely, adverse childhood experiences that cause low self-esteem would include being harshly criticized, humiliated, sexually or emotionally abused, ignored, or expected to be "perfect" all the time.

We all have inner dialogues that support or reinforce our beliefs and expectations. When we open any number of social-media platforms and scroll through photos of vacations, celebrations with family and friends, and adorable pets, our inner critic might say, "I'm not successful enough" or "I'm not good enough." When there's a constant stream of such information, for the anxiously and avoidantly attached person, it becomes increasingly difficult to stave off feelings of inadequacy or inferiority; their inner critic is harsh and destructive and undermines their self-esteem.

SKILL-BUILDING STRATEGIES

How do you raise your self-esteem? Below are some suggestions.

- Try not to be overly critical of yourself or demand perfection. Work on being more patient with yourself and others, developing self-compassion, expressing emotions, and being open to trying varied interests and new activities. These actions are *big* steps toward raising your self-esteem.
- Avoid derogatory self-talk. While an occasional self-disparaging comment is normal, recurrent and chronic negative remarks about yourself are symptoms of low self-esteem. We all have our strengths and weaknesses. Just like we cannot all be great at everything, the opposite is also true—we *cannot* all be bad at everything. Generalizing negative beliefs about ourselves inhibits us from having a realistic picture of our true abilities. Take time out to think of a few things you are not "terrible" at and that you might even enjoy doing. Most likely, your list will be longer than you expected. Make a plan to do one of the things on your list. Doing activities you feel good about will naturally build your self-esteem.
- Develop relationships with a healthy dependency. When we feel a combination of both connection and independence in our relationships, we have established a healthy dependency. These types of relationships empower us to take risks, to venture out and explore new relationships and interests, *and*, at the same time, to feel connected and close to the essential people in our lives.
- Give yourself permission to ask for help. Talking with a mental-health professional can help you learn to raise your self-esteem in a supportive and emotionally secure environment.

BACK TO JOANNE

In time, as our therapeutic sessions continued, Joanne began to talk about her genuine feelings of sadness related to her oldest daughter's imminent departure for college.

> I never got the chance to know my mom before she died eight years ago. My mom kept her feelings hidden, and we weren't a close family. Even now I rarely see or talk to my brother and two sisters. I'm afraid I've repeated the same relationship I had with my family with my kids and my husband. I feel as though I'm running out of time to fix things. And I don't have many friends or outside interests. I learned to downplay having close relationships from my parents. And I'm starting to understand that my misuse of social media is not the healthiest way for me to distract myself from my feelings about my past, present, and future.

Avoidantly attached individuals like Joanne are less likely to reveal their vulnerable selves. As discussed in chapter 1, self-disclosure is a necessity for cultivating emotional intimacy in our relationships. She had learned to suppress her feelings and downplay her emotional distress. This pattern became evident to me when she first talked to me about her relationship with her daughter. But later in our therapeutic sessions, Joanne was able to express her true feelings—and the regret she felt about not having an emotionally close relationship with her daughter, her son, and her husband.

Research examining the link between social media and avoidant attachment style suggests that avoidantly attached individuals inflate their positive self-views. They do this by underreporting feelings of intense emotion, concealing what they consider to be negative aspects of themselves to promote a positive self-image, and rarely posting personal information,[9] like posting a family picture or a comment about having a tough day at the office. Furthermore, as previously mentioned, research studies investigating social media and emotional well-being also suggest that we all feel worse, regardless of attachment style, when we passively consume social media. Since avoidantly attached individuals are more likely to passively participate on social-media platforms, by scrolling through newsfeeds rather than interacting with their virtual friends, one could assume that social media across the board negatively impacts their emotional health.

Most of the work Joanne and I did in session was around helping her understand how her past influenced her current relationship style, which was characteristic of an avoidant attachment. Examining her history also allowed Joanne to get more comfortable with talking about and processing complicated feelings. Joanne stated that for the first time she felt able to share with me not just her feelings and thoughts but her hopes and dreams as well.

Over time, Joanne developed a closer relationship with her daughter, her son, and her husband. She was also excited about the possibility of using social media as a way of staying in touch with her daughter while she was away at college. She and her daughter even agreed to FaceTime once a week. Joanne also began to feel more comfortable using social media as a way to socialize and stay in touch with old friends. She even posted a few pictures of her and her family from her daughter's graduation.

A few weeks after her daughter graduated, Joanne came to my office, particularly happy and bubbly. "I think I've made some new friends," she said. "Remember how I told you I posted a picture of our family taken at my daughter's graduation on Facebook? A few of the moms from my daughter's school liked my picture, and one mom posted a comment suggesting we start a book club in the fall. I love to read, and it'll be a great way for me to make friends!"

FINDING SAFE PLACES ONLINE

As we've learned in this chapter, our earliest relationships determine our attachment style, and our attachment style dramatically impacts the quality of our life. It influences how well we're able to relate to others and regulate our emotions, our cognition, and our behaviors. And, as we're learning, our attachment style also impacts how we use social media, why we use social media, and what we hope to gain from it. For example, does social media enhance our relationships, or does it cause more emotional distress, bringing about conflicts or disagreements played out online? Have you ever tried quitting social media by deactivating your accounts or ever tried going on a detox diet because of a social-media influencer's impact on you?

Finding emotionally safe digital spaces and striking a healthy balance in the digital age is challenging, and our attachment style likely has something to do with how successful we will be with finding emotional safety in the digital era. Below are a few recommendations to help you find balance and psychological safety in the digital age through the lens of attachment.

RECOMMENDATIONS

1. Figure out your attachment style. You can start by examining how you feel in your relationships. For example, do you feel secure with others? Do you fear being rejected by those close to you? Are you preoccupied with how others perceive you? Do you view yourself as more of a solitary person, not needing close connections? Remember, securely attached individuals feel safe and secure in their relationships and enjoy reciprocal connections. Anxiously attached individuals are preoccupied with how others perceive them and seek out reassurance from others. Avoidantly attached individuals downplay the importance of relationships. Having a better understanding of your attachment style is the first step to finding a safe space both online and offline.

2. When you find yourself using social media, ask yourself, "Why am I doing this?" Is it because you're feeling sad, bored, or lonely? Or is it to connect with friends and family? Once you determine what you are looking for, you can then set realistic goals for what kind of role social media will play in forming relationships and you can make sure you're not using it in a self-sabotaging way. Remember, our attachments are primarily formed by our in-person interactions.

3. Seek professional help if your attachment style is causing you emotional harm and your relationships to suffer. It's estimated that only 60 percent of adults are securely attached. Our attachment styles affect everything relational in our lives, from the partners we choose to how well every relationship we have will progress and even how they will end. Talking to a mental-health

professional can help us understand our strengths and vulnerabilities in the context of attachment so we can develop healthier relationships.

3

THE DISTORTED MIRROR

No one can make you feel inferior without your consent.
—attributed to Eleanor Roosevelt

Recently while in a yoga class that I hadn't been to before, I caught myself deep in a thought loop of destructive social comparisons: "Am I as flexible as the person next to me, behind me, or even across the room from me? Do I have as much experience as the other people in the class? Am I as in shape as the other women my age?" I was surprised by the extent to which these thoughts affected my self-confidence. They slowed me down and loomed over me for a good bit of the class. Most people aren't aware of the degree to which social comparisons affect them, yet research shows we're always evaluating our abilities and comparing ourselves to those around us.

We usually think nothing good can come from social comparisons, but you might be surprised to learn that measuring ourselves against others can be helpful and even lead to emotional and personal development. For example, the inspiration you feel about someone else's achievements can motivate you to improve your own life. On the flip side, however, social comparisons can bring to the surface deep-seated feelings of resentment, envy, shame, and inadequacy, turning your mood upside down. They can stunt your emotional growth, exacerbate depression and anxiety, and destroy relationships.

In this chapter you'll learn about the psychological and biological roots underlying our drive to formulate social comparisons and how to recognize the two main types: upward comparisons and downward comparisons. I'll present case studies of two people who secretly compare themselves to others in real life and online. The chapter concludes with techniques you can immediately implement in your life in order to gain better control over destructive envy and self-doubt that can be triggered by social media and real-life comparisons. You will learn strategies such as cultivating balanced thinking, identifying and managing a tendency to overly idealize other people's posts, and educating yourself about the dangers of passively consuming social media.

THE NUTS AND BOLTS OF SOCIAL COMPARISON

Increasingly in my practice, I hear things like,

> "I wish I had my best friend's life! Her family always travels to amazing places, she gets the best clothing, and she's a top student and athlete. Her pictures on Instagram and Facebook prove it!"
> "I was constantly compared to my brother growing up. He was the smart son, the cool son, the cute son. I guess that's why I feel so envious of him now. He doesn't know it, but I unfollowed him on Facebook because I got so angry after seeing posts of his charmed life."
> "Seeing pictures of my ex-boyfriend's girlfriend on social media never takes me to a good place. I constantly compare myself to her in every way—looks, career, kids, finances, and friends. You name it, and I've compared it!"

Do you frequently compare yourself to others in real life or on social media? If so, you're not alone! Dr. Leon Festinger, a psychologist well known for his social-comparison theory, found that people have an innate drive to evaluate their abilities and opinions. In fact, by doing so, we gain important information about ourselves like, "Am I a good person or a bad person?" "Do people like me?" or "Am I successful?" More specifically, comparisons that let us know how good we are at a particular skill or talent—like running, math, or art—can lead to emotional and personal development by inspiring us and motivating us to improve. Comparing a particular circumstance in our life to someone else— "What can I learn from my friend who just landed her dream job?"— can be similarly useful. Comparisons can even help us feel better about our decisions and ourselves: "I might not be rich like my best friend, but he just went through a bitter divorce, and I'm happily married."

Festinger also states that when objective, nonsocial standards for comparisons are unavailable, people will make comparisons with those most similar to themselves in background, age, intelligence, attractiveness, wealth, and success. This means we're most likely to compare ourselves to our friends, neighbors, colleagues, family members, and, not surprisingly, virtual friends we follow when nonsocial standards aren't available or appropriate.[1] We're less likely to compare ourselves to people who are more dissimilar to us. For example, when I was in my yoga class, I did not compare myself to the experienced and well-trained yoga instructor. However, the danger in all comparisons is their potential to produce what's known as *upward comparisons* and *downward comparisons*, both of which have a big impact on our well-being and self-esteem.

First, let's unpack what exactly upward comparisons and downward comparisons are and how they impact our emotional health and self-esteem.

WHAT ARE UPWARD COMPARISONS?

Upward comparisons are made when we compare ourselves to people we believe are better than or superior to us. For instance, we might believe an acquaintance is more attractive or more financially successful than we are. Not surprisingly, upward comparisons can hurt our self-confidence by triggering deep-seated feelings of resentment, envy, and shame. Upward comparisons can contribute to or exacerbate depression and anxiety and can even sabotage our relationships.[2]

WHAT ARE DOWNWARD COMPARISONS?

Conversely, downward comparisons happen when we make comparisons with others we believe to be inferior or less than us. Downward comparisons can boost self-image and enhance self-esteem because they produce feelings of superiority over another person.[3] However, downward comparisons are made at the cost of another's misfortune or by diminishing or devaluing an individual or group. It's not hard to imagine how using downward comparisons as a means for coping with, for example, low self-esteem could damage relationships and inhibit emotional growth.

MEET JAMES, AN UPWARD-COMPARISON SOCIAL MEDIA USER

James is in his early thirties and is the father of an eight-year-old son. He recently separated from his girlfriend of nine years, the mother of his son. In sessions, James often laments over his compulsive need to make upward comparisons.

> I have a bad habit of comparing myself to other guys and thinking they are so much better than me. When I'm at my son's sports games or at one of his school activities, I automatically start comparing myself to other dads. I compare our appearance, our careers, our homes, our cars, and even our kids' achievements. It's gotten to the point where I get worked up days before I'm supposed to be at an event for my son, and at the event, I get so caught up in negative thoughts that I completely tune out what my son is doing and why I'm there! I'm missing out on watching my son grow up. He's my whole life!

James acknowledged that social media is another arena in which he compares himself to other men like himself.

> Being on social media is so self-destructive for me. I always end up feeling worse after logging on. The truth is, so many of my friends post pictures of their families, their girlfriends, and their cool trips. Since my breakup, finances have been tight, and I haven't traveled much. I spend less time with my son because of shared custody. I feel awful about myself when I see all the other dads with their kids, wives, or girlfriends. I'm tired of always feeling that everyone has it so much better than me and that something is missing from my life. I literally feel like I'm broken inside.

Not only do sites like Facebook and Instagram provide us with an endless supply of social-comparison opportunities, but we can also access them anytime and anywhere, making our natural drive to compare ourselves to others hard to keep at bay. Social comparisons that take place online are unique in the sense that they almost exclusively evoke upward comparison—those comparisons with others who are seemingly doing better than us.[4] This is because on social media people tend to showcase the very best versions of themselves and share only the highlights of their lives. Rarely does someone post about what went wrong on their vacation or about the family fight that broke out right before that "perfect" holiday family picture. The idyllic representations of others can naturally give us the feeling that something is wrong with our own lives, triggering emotions such as fear of missing out (FOMO), shame, and self-doubt.

Over time, in our sessions together, it became clear that James's compulsive upward social comparisons were feeding his vulnerability to envy others.

ENVY, A BY-PRODUCT OF UPWARD COMPARISONS

Envy is a normal human emotion. We feel envious when we want what another person has, like fame, fortune, or power. Envy is different from jealousy; we feel jealous when we are afraid someone will take from us something we already have that's important to us, such as a romantic partner, best friend, or job.[5]

Envious feelings aren't only triggered by material possessions. We can also envy people in our community and social circle and even family members who are admired, influential, and successful. We all know how bad it feels when we're envious of someone else. Sometimes our envious feelings manifest as hostility or anger. At other times our envious feelings manifest as shame and inferiority. Most people work hard to hide their envious feelings, especially from the very people they envy.

Envy has long been of interest and regarded as an important emotion in psychoanalytic theory and practice. Melanie Klein, a psychoanalyst from the early twentieth century who was influenced by the work of Sigmund Freud, wrote about envy and its potentially destructive consequences. Klein believed envy to be an innate or biological "expression of destructive impulses," meaning it is present from birth, and that it has a "constitutional basis." In addition to seeing envy as the product of angry feelings from what another person possesses and enjoys, Klein also believed that envious feelings are sometimes accompanied by "an impulse to take away or spoil" whatever it is one envies. It is in the acting out of the wish to spoil the goodness of the person envied that this emotion can be destructive and pathological.[6]

Most of us are familiar with the sort of person whose envious feelings are "acted out" in ways that are designed to be hurtful and diminishing. For example, an envious friend or family member might make a disparaging remark about a recent accomplishment you mentioned. A more destructive envious person might attempt to spoil another's accomplishment or success by constructing ways to cause that person grief or emotional harm.

SKILL-BUILDING STRATEGIES

Being envious is normal; we all feel it from time to time. However, persistent envious feelings contribute greatly to depression, global feelings of dissatisfaction, and unhappiness and wreak havoc on our relationships. So the question is, how can examining our envious feelings help us? Below are four tips to help you find the positive side of envy.

- Be honest with yourself about your envious feelings. Most of us do not want to admit that we have envious feelings toward another person. However, it's important to remind ourselves that envy is a normal emotion. Write a list of what exactly it is you envy about a particular person.
- Interpret your envious feelings as an opportunity for personal growth. Examining who and what causes you to feel envious can lead to self-awareness. Remember, you would not feel as strongly about the person you envy if whatever they have weren't also important to or a priority for you.
- Avoid or minimize social media when feeling bad or facing adversity. Part of our self-esteem is determined by how well we measure up on our social comparisons. For example, if

we meet our expectations and goals, we feel excited about life and good about ourselves. When we aren't meeting our goals or when we are facing adversity such as going through a divorce or losing a job, we're bound to feel depressed or even ashamed. At these times, we're also more apt to make social comparisons.

- Gain a realistic perspective of social media. It's normal for us to showcase our achievements and the highlights of our lives. This is part of the human condition. But no matter how wonderful a person's life might appear on social media, life has its down moments for everyone.

BACK TO JAMES

"Lately, I've been envious of my best friend, Drake," James told me one day in session.

> Our lives are pretty similar. He separated from his wife around the same time my girlfriend and I broke up, and he has a son about my kid's age. His posts on Facebook and Instagram make me feel terrible about myself! He just started seeing a gorgeous woman he met on a dating app, but I haven't had any luck dating. His son is popular and great at basketball, but my son isn't a strong athlete, and he's struggling socially at school. Drake is a big social media user. When I log on, I only intend to scroll through my newsfeed for a few minutes, but I see all of his posts and lose track of time. I know I have to stay away from social media, but it is hard to do!

One of the most destructive effects of upward social comparisons is that it kills self-confidence and self-esteem. James's upward comparisons left him feeling like his life was inferior in every way. They also made him feel as if he were incapable of making good decisions for himself. When he saw pictures of his friends on social media or read updates, more times than not he was left with a sinking feeling that his life was lacking.

Over the course of treatment, James worked on gaining an awareness of the emotions driving his habit of upward comparison. Adversities, like a big breakup or divorce, can trigger envious feelings. James's upward comparisons with Drake and the other dads distracted him from acknowledging his deeper feelings of loss, powerlessness, fear, and resentment brought on by his girlfriend's decision to end their nine-year relationship. James worked hard to learn how to look inward rather than outward and how to pay attention and listen to his emotions. Our emotions shape who we are and guide our lives. Where and how we direct our energy is where our life will go.

Over time, as I got to know James better, I learned that he had a very supportive family. James was especially close to his older brother, whom he said was always available to listen and as a shoulder to lean on. As James talked more and more about the details of his life, he realized that his life wasn't all bad—and neither was he.

"I'm going through a really tough time right now," he told me, "but I now know my life isn't a total disaster. I have a great son and a pretty decent job. Appreciating the good things in my life is helping me get through my separation. I feel more hopeful about my future. I know I won't feel bad forever."

The fact is, there is no one else in the world or even the history of the world, including Drake, who has the exact same family, childhood, or interests and passions as James. And of course, no one has or ever will have the exact same DNA or genetic code. When each of us, like James, recognizes and embraces what makes us unique and special, we begin to develop gratitude.

GRATITUDE: THE ANTIDOTE TO ENVY

The benefits of practicing gratitude are plentiful. Robert Emmons, a psychologist and leading scientific expert on the science of gratitude, says gratitude blocks toxic emotions, such as envy, resentment, regret, and depression, and that it's impossible to feel envious and grateful at the same time. Gratitude works because it allows us to celebrate the present and be an active participant in our own lives. Valuing and appreciating friends, oneself, situations, and circumstances focuses the mind on what we already have rather than on something that's absent and is needed, Emmons says.[7]

In a nutshell, studies show that people who regularly practice gratitude by noticing and reflecting on the things for which they are thankful enjoy many benefits, including

- More joyful emotions
- Fewer incidents of anxiety and depression
- Feeling more engaged in their lives
- Sleeping better
- More compassion and
- More fulfilling relationships.

Gratitude, according to psychoanalyst Melanie Klein, has the ability to dampen pathological envy. Like envy, gratitude, Klein says, is inborn and a crucial component of our ability to perceive the goodness in other people. She also feels that cultivating gratitude during our early years directly impacts our capacity for love in subsequent love relationships throughout life.

James had a lot to be grateful for. He had a loving, caring, and supportive family. He had a good relationship with his son. A few years ago, he'd suffered a health scare that, fortunately, turned out to be okay, but now he was healthy—certainly something to be grateful for.

Along with helping James learn to be grateful for the big things in his life, our sessions together helped him experience the same level of gratitude for the simple and smaller things in his life. Simply put, gratitude reminds us of the simple joy of just being alive.

SKILL-BUILDING STRATEGIES

Making any big life change is hard, and finding the motivation and stick-to-itiveness to sustain it can be challenging. By cultivating gratitude, you can better see the gifts you already have, which can make navigating the changes feel a little less daunting. Below are a few strategies to help you start and maintain a daily practice of gratitude.

- Strengthen your reflection skills. One of the cornerstones of the practice of gratitude is being able to recognize the things we are grateful for. You can strengthen your reflection skills by noticing all the new things you're grateful for every day and then writing them down in a gratitude journal or on a piece of paper to put in a special gratitude jar or box. Periodically read what you've written to remind yourself of all the things you're grateful for.
- Be specific about what you're grateful for—for example, "I'm grateful for having my cute, cuddly, and affectionate dog" or "I'm grateful that I'm healthy and my body doesn't have any aches or pains."
- Make a point to follow people and accounts on social media that foster feelings of gratitude within you. For example, there are tons of Twitter users devoted to posting motivational messages, articles, and advice. Find them. Follow them. Retweet them. Connect with them.
- Share your feelings of gratitude. Include the important people in your life in your gratitude practice. You can do this by writing letters or sending e-mails to the people in your life for whom you're grateful or by making a point to directly express your feelings of gratitude in person. However you choose to express your gratitude to the people you love, focusing on our relationships enhances feelings of connection and intimacy. Time after time, studies have shown that our relationships are strong determinants of our happiness.

MEET SUZANNE, A DOWNWARD-COMPARISON SOCIAL MEDIA USER

Suzanne came to see me at her mother's urging. Her mom was worried about Suzanne's dramatic changes in mood and behaviors over the past year. Suzanne was doing poorly in school. She was barely getting by. She was also withdrawing from her friends and family and was getting into frequent arguments with Cameron, her girlfriend since her sophomore year in high school. They'd gotten along well, for the most part, until just a few months ago. Suzanne was a senior in high school when we first met, and she was getting ready to apply to college.

"Since my grades aren't good, I'm not going to get into a great college like most of my friends and my girlfriend, Cameron," Suzanne told me one day in session.

> Cameron is very smart. I'm sure she'll get into her first choice. She works hard, so she deserves it. We've been dating for two years, but recently it's gotten hard to be around her. I find myself being overly critical. I criticize her appearance, the people she hangs out with, and the activities she does to boost her college application. Deep down, I know I'm picking fights with her because I'm evnious that she seems to have a brighter future than I do. I want her to feel worse than me so that I can feel better than her. I haven't posted anything on social media in weeks, but I do occasionally log on and scroll through my friends' posts. Sometimes I post sarcastic comments to make myself feel better.

Suzanne was right. She probably would not get into one of her top college choices. Yet she still had the time and the potential to improve her circumstances. In order for Suzanne to get to a place where she could grow emotionally, she had to acknowledge rather than repress her feelings of envy and inadequacy. She also had to work on realizing that her use of downward comparisons, through diminishing her friends' achievements and devaluing them as individuals, was an unhealthy defense mechanism. Rather than neutralizing her envious feelings, she needed to acknowledge them and see how they were holding her back from growing emotionally and from pursuing her dreams.

Underneath Suzanne's drive to feel superior by making downward comparisons with Cameron and other people was her wish to hide and not feel "broken inside." Unfortunately, by maintaining a false sense of superiority, Suzanne was pushing away the very people who loved her the most and could potentially help her. It was also using up mental energy she could have put toward improving her circumstances.

With lots of time, patience, and work, Suzanne began to feel safe and strong enough to examine her envious feelings without the need to "cut down" others. She decided to take a gap year between high school and college, during which she signed up for a few college classes; and she did really well in them. The following year, Suzanne applied to schools that she felt were challenging but attainable, which would bolster her self-esteem. A few years ago, I received a letter from Suzanne letting me know she had graduated from college and was pursuing a career in a field she loved and, most importantly, was proud of!

THE PERILS OF FOMO

As we're learning, social media is a hotbed for social comparisons. The phenomenon of FOMO—or the fear of missing out—refers to the apprehension that we are either not in-the-know or that our life is lacking particular social events, experiences, or interactions.[8] FOMO, idealization (attributing overly positive qualities to another person or thing), and devaluation (exaggerating the negative attributes of an object or another person by seeing them or it as completely flawed and worthless) are forms of what is known as *cognitive distortion*. Cognitive distortions are simply ways that our mind convinces us of something that isn't really true. Cognitive distortions are thoughts that reinforce our negative emotions—when we tell ourselves things that sound rational and accurate but only serve to keep us feeling bad about ourselves.

We will examine cognitive distortion in more depth in chapter 6.

FOMO can also lead to what's called *black-and-white thinking*—also known as *polarized* or *all-or-nothing thinking*—which occurs when we process people and circumstances as either "all good" or "all bad." An example of polarized thinking is, "I'm a complete failure, while my sister is a complete success" or "He's perfect at everything he does, and I'm a total klutz" or "I'm unlucky all the time, while my best friend is always lucky." In a nutshell, black-and-white thinking oversimplifies the fact that people are complex and life is complicated. The more polarized a person's thinking, the more vulnerable they are to the downside of social comparisons both online and in real life, which leads to feelings like inferiority, a false sense of superiority, and depression.[9]

Social-media content is highly controlled and reveals to its consumers only bits and pieces of another person's life and experiences, making black-and-white thinking more likely. In reality, if we aren't in personal contact with those we follow, we truly have no way of knowing what their life was like before they posted or afterward. Social media or any virtual encounter cannot replace the fuller and richer human experience one gains from in-person interactions. Eye contact, the human voice, touch, flowing conversation, emotional intimacy, and appreciation of another's essence cannot be replicated by virtual encounters. Plus, studies show that having frequent interactions with friends and family combats symptoms of depression and anxiety.[10]

SKILL-BUILDING STRATEGIES

The truth is, for most people, things aren't completely horrible or completely wonderful. They fall somewhere in the middle—in life's gray zone. Slowing down to think and feel in the gray zone can be immensely helpful in countering cognitive distortions such as black-and-white thinking.

- Avoid absolutes. *Always, impossible, ruined, never, perfect, terrible*, and *disastrous* are absolutes and not at all helpful in understanding relationships or situations that are complex and involve mixed feelings. Cultivate self-talk that's compassionate and forgiving, such as, "It's good enough" and "There is no such thing as perfect."
- Work on becoming less rigid in your thinking. Challenge your thoughts. Ask yourself, "Is it possible to be a generally intelligent person but not proficient in everything?" Or "Can what I'm facing be difficult now but get better in time?"
- Accept the fact that no one is perfect. We're all human; we all make mistakes. Try to see the value in learning from our mistakes.
- Learn to physically relax and cognitively slow down. Black-and-white thinking spikes when emotions are high. Breathe slowly, and use relaxation techniques to curb emotional arousal and allow your more rational self to take over.

WHAT TO DO NOW

We now know that drawing social comparisons is a part of being human. We all do it, whether or not we're conscious of or admit to it. Although drawing social comparisons can be positive for our self-development and emotional growth by providing us with inspiration, not everyone fares well when drawing social comparisons. For some, they bring about emotional pain by stirring up self-destructive feelings of envy, shame, and inadequacy, destroying the cultivation of healthy self-esteem and hope.

In my personal and professional experience, social comparisons that harm our emotional well-being rarely, if ever, have a positive impact. They don't snap us into feeling better, and neither do they force us to make life-changing decisions that dramatically improve our lives. Rather, harmful social comparisons, like upward and downward comparisons, can trick our brains into believing that leading our best lives comes from looking outside of ourselves rather than within. The idea that negative social comparisons can act as a catalyst for positive change is a terrible misconception, because it denies the reality that we are all unique individuals, with our own unique set of strengths, talents, and, yes, *weaknesses*. So, what is right for one person will rarely be exactly what is right for another. Chasing someone else's life and talents stops us all from pursuing our own dreams and living our best lives.

RECOMMENDATIONS

1. Tune in to your emotions. Develop the ability to recognize and label emotions, such as envy, jealousy, and longing. Compulsively comparing yourself to someone else distracts from acknowledging your own feelings and puts distance between you and your solutions. Gaining self-awareness through reflection improves self-
understanding, which is key for making the changes that are just right for you. Schedule regular times for self-reflection by setting aside time in your day to write in a journal or meditate.
2. Minimize time on social media, or completely avoid it altogether. If you find yourself more times than not feeling worse about your

life's course after logging on to social media, take a break from it. As we now know, social media naturally instigates feelings of envy, FOMO, inferiority, and feeling as though one's life is lacking. Beware of the dangers of black-and-white thinking and its impact on how you feel when consuming social media of any kind.

3. Practice gratitude. Learn to appreciate all the good that is in your life, especially your own unique strengths and talents. Being grateful not only helps tame negative feelings brought about by social comparisons on social media and in our real-life relationships, but it also gives us a healthier perspective, leading to a truly authentic, fuller life!

4

SUBSTANCE ABUSE, DEPRESSION, BODY IMAGE, AND THE IMPORTANCE OF SOCIAL MEDIA LITERACY

When we are no longer able to change a situation . . . we are challenged to change ourselves.

—Viktor Frankl[1]

Psychologists and social scientists know that social media can trigger feelings of "compare and despair," envy, shame, guilt, and low self-esteem. It can worsen many mental-health disorders; alarmingly, for some this worsening has taken the form of a crisis. Since the ubiquitous use of social media, the rise in numbers of those who have died by suicide between the ages of ten to twenty-four years has jumped 56 percent from 2007 to 2017.[2]

If you or someone you know is having suicidal thoughts, it is important that you get them immediate care through a hospital or mental-health facility. The National Suicide Prevention Lifeline is 1-800-273-8255. It's available twenty-four hours a day, seven days a week.

Most of the time, the impact of social media on mental health is less critical but more insidious and no less important to address. In particular, in my practice I have seen a clear and direct increase in the part social media plays in the manifestation of four mental-health issues: depression, anxiety, body-image disorders, and substance-abuse disorders.

People struggling with depression and anxiety have a harder time than their nondepressed and nonanxious counterparts shaking off the negative feelings and thoughts brought on by social-media use. For those who are struggling to feel comfortable in their bodies, seeing images of unrealistic "picture-perfect" women can bring on and trigger episodes of self-loathing or binge-and-purge eating. Finally, social media can trigger individuals working on living a sober life into urges to relapse.

The good news is that you can strive to lessen social media's impact on these disorders by educating yourself about the importance of developing social-media literacy. Simply put, *social-media literacy* is the ability to process the knowledge and beliefs we gather from consuming social media through the lens of critical thinking.[3] Critical thinking is important because it allows us to realistically evaluate the information we read, see, and take in from our social-media use. Social-media literacy gives us the skills to apply multidimensional thinking to a one-dimensional social-media world—in other words, to appreciate the complexities of life regardless of what quotation, picture, article, or post is being circulated on the Internet. In this way, the skills associated with social-media literacy are similar to those associated with cognitive behavioral therapy (CBT) and dialectical behavioral therapy (DBT). Like DBT and CBT, social-media literacy seeks to help the consumer use social media in ways that are skillful and life enhancing, reducing the risk of experiencing aftereffects that can make life worse.

In this chapter you'll meet Leo, a newly recovering substance abuser and social-media user and Olivia, a social-media user struggling with body-image issues. You'll also learn about key concepts associated with CBT and DBT that can be used to minimize triggers brought on by social-media use.

But first, let's begin by defining *emotional health*.

EMOTIONAL HEALTH

What does it mean to be emotionally healthy? There may seem to be an obvious answer to this question, but emotional health is actually a multifaceted concept. To begin with, emotional health refers to our overall psychological well-being. This includes the way we feel about ourselves (self-esteem), the quality of our relationships (degree of meaningful relationships), how well we are able to modulate and work through difficult feelings—such as anger, disappointment, and frustration (regulating and letting go of negative emotions)—and our ability to cope with difficult circumstances (our level of grit and resilience). In short, people who are emotionally healthy feel in control of their emotions and behaviors, have positive and strong relationships, and recover from setbacks.

Being emotionally healthy does not mean being happy all the time. Everyone will experience loss and disappointment and undergo difficult, unexpected transitions at some point, and everyone will have periods of sadness, anxiety, and stress. This is normal. This is life. Emotionally healthy people feel stressed and sad, too. What differentiates them from their emotionally unhealthy counterparts is that emotionally healthy people are fully aware of and conscious of their negative feelings. Therefore, emotionally healthy individuals do not deny, distort, displace, project, repress, or avoid difficult and painful emotions like sadness, fear, disappointment, uncertainty, anger, or embarrassment. Studies show that emotional health is a learned skill, and they stress the importance of actively working to maintain our emotional health at every stage of life, from childhood to adolescence and through adulthood and old age.[4]

Everything we do, what we expose ourselves to, and how we choose to spend our time significantly impacts our emotional health. Not surprisingly, this includes the Netflix shows we watch, the games we play on our phones, our hobbies or lack thereof, the books we read, what we eat and drink, the people we bring into our lives, and the social-media accounts and profiles we follow. Below I discuss the power of social-media literacy to mitigate symptoms associated with three mental-health issues outlined in this chapter: substance abuse, depression, and body-image disorders.

HOW SOCIAL MEDIA LITERACY HELPS US STAY EMOTIONALLY HEALTH IN THE DIGITAL AGE

What exactly is *social-media literacy*? How can social-media literacy help us stay emotionally healthy in the digital age? And how can it help those struggling with depression, anxiety, substance abuse, an eating disorder, or any other type of mental-health issue stay on track?

Merriam-Webster defines *literacy* as the ability to read and write and as having knowledge or competence—the traditional definition of literacy as applied to the printed word. However, with the advent of the World Wide Web, the Internet, and social media, our literacy can also be measured as it relates to our knowledge of and competence navigating media. Having media literacy entails having the ability to access, analyze, evaluate, create, and act using all forms of digital communication. Living in the digital age allows anyone to create any form of media. From text messages and advertising to memes and viral content, media takes all shapes and forms. This is why social-media literacy is important.

At the forefront of social-media literacy is the concept of critical-thinking skills. Cultivating critical thinking in the digital era is especially important for children, adolescents, and young adults, considering the amount of content they consume on a minute-by-minute basis. Skillfully being able to evaluate any type of digital media, including social media, means having the ability to determine what information is pertinent and what content may be excluded and being able to accurately interpret the overall message and purpose of a text, picture, or post. These skills make us less vulnerable to being seduced into falling for misrepresentations and fabrications of reality.

Being aware of our emotions while we're logged on to social media is another important aspect of media literacy. Asking ourselves questions such as, "What was I feeling or doing before I decided to log on?" "How do I feel while scrolling on social media, surfing the Web, or watching YouTube?" and "Why am I feeling this way now?" are all very important considerations to contemplate while logging on.

Finally, social-media literacy entails the awareness of social media's impact on us individually and on our society. To explain further, there's no doubt that social media has forever changed the way we think about the world, each other, and ourselves. Social media is not only a digital space that allows us to connect with family, friends, and people from all over the world, it is also an information hub, shaping and reinforcing our attitudes, behaviors, preoccupations, and ideas. We now log on to catch up with the news, follow the financial markets, keep current regarding cultural trends, and follow the lives of celebrities, athletes, and thought leaders. There's no doubt about it, social media has the real ability to influence our decisions, our actions, our behaviors, our political opinions, where we should travel, and what schools our kids should attend. Challenging the messages telegraphed via social media requires a strong grasp of social-media literacy.

Let's now turn our attention to Leo, a social-media user in recovery from alcohol abuse. We'll explore how social-media literacy helps him to stay on the path to recovery.

MEET LEO, A NEWLY RECOVERING SUBSTANCE ABUSER AND SOCIAL-MEDIA USER

Leo was four weeks sober when he first came to see me for help with living a sober lifestyle. He was twenty-two years old, had recently graduated from college, and was living at home with his parents. He had just gotten discharged from an inpatient-rehabilitation program when we began our work together.

College had been a difficult transition for Leo. He had struggled with navigating his new independence and with sticking to a schedule without his parents' constant oversight. As a result, Leo found himself partying more than studying or attending classes. "I had a really hard time managing my schedule and finding a healthy balance between being social and studying," Leo told me in session.

> When I was in college, I was going out almost every night, getting stone-cold drunk, but most of my friends were only partying two to three times a week, and they weren't getting hammered every time they went out.
>
> I'm not proud to admit this, but more times than I can count on my two hands I blacked out from drinking too much. Now that I'm in recovery and thinking straight, I'm lucky to be alive and that I didn't die from alcohol poisoning. I tried keeping my drinking a secret from my friends, my parents, and even myself by minimizing it and pretending that the stupid things I did when I was drunk were funny and intentional. But in reality, the things I did when I was drunk scared me, and I didn't know how to stop drinking.

Shortly after Leo moved back home after graduating from college, his parents quickly realized that their son's drinking was beyond just normal young-adult antics. Luckily, when they sat down and confronted Leo about their concerns, Leo realized his drinking and partying had crossed a line, and he was ready to work on getting sober.

"Staying sober is harder than I ever thought it would be," Leo continued. "I'm twenty-two years old. Most of what people my age do for fun is go to parties, bars, and concerts. It goes without saying that 99 percent of the time drinking is involved. I'm trying hard to build friendships with other sober people my age, but it takes time. I don't just want to cut off the friendships I have with all the people I met at college and friends I've known since I was really little too."

It's estimated that 19.7 million Americans twelve years and older are battling a substance-use disorder, and of that group, 74 percent are primarily struggling with alcoholism.[5] Frequent alcohol use over time literally rewires the brain's reward patterns. This means that those abusing alcohol develop a destructive set of behavioral responses and associations, formed from deeply ingrained habits, telling them that drinking alcohol leads to rewarding experiences. This makes for a difficult and tenacious behavior and emotional association to break.[6]

In treatment, Leo worked hard on identifying his triggers—more specifically, the people, places, and things that made him more likely to have an urge to drink, setting him up for a relapse. Whenever I'm working with someone in recovery, one of the very first treatment goals we set involves devising a plan of action to avoid succumbing to tempting alcohol-abuse triggers. For Leo that meant working with him to identify and anticipate alcohol triggers, being able to recognize them in their early stages, and developing strategies to reduce their power over his behavior.

Leo recognized that his coping mechanisms were severely compromised and that even after completing twenty-eight days of an in-patient treatment program, his old habits remained tenacious. One of his most tenacious habits was social-media use.

> People my age, me included, see social media and our smartphones as lifelines. But now social media is one of my triggers for me, because so many people I follow post pictures of themselves out partying and drinking. I can't help but feel left out and that I'm missing out on being with my friends when I'm scrolling through Instagram,

viewing Snapchat, and on the rare occasion [when] I look at my Facebook account.

I know I'm not ready to be around alcohol, so I'm keeping my distance from seeing these friends in real life, but to be honest, the thought of picking up ramps up after being on social media. I don't want to completely shut down from social media and cut off social-media ties with my friends that still drink.

In many, ways Leo was right: As social beings, our social relationships are crucial to our well-being. And for Leo, growing up with social media and the Internet meant social media was an integral part of his social network and support system.

As far as social media's potential destructive consequences for a person's recovery, it's not hard to see how scrolling through Facebook and Instagram, seeing photos of friends drinking and out having fun, can trigger unwanted cravings—for example, by stirring up a fear of missing out from being sober. Additionally, virtual triggers are alarmingly similar to real-life triggers: Being in a social setting where there's alcohol—such as at a bar, a party, or any event where alcohol is served—or running into drinking buddies can trigger the faulty wiring in the brain that links drinking to pleasurable experiences and makes us only remember the good times we had when drinking or using other substances. Just so, seeing mere *pictures* that conjure up these memories on social media has the exact same effect. Social media's powerful emotional impact should not be underestimated as a real potential trigger for those in recovery.

Leo needed to develop a way of making social media work for him—using it in a way that supported his recovery and helped him to build positive relationships while at the same time maintaining his established friendships that were already positive and healing.

Over the many months Leo was in treatment, he worked hard on boiling down how he was triggered and which people were triggers for him on social media. He and I then worked on devising a plan for how to use social media in ways that diffused his triggers. Through lots of trial and error, Leo discovered that he could best maintain a healthy online presence after editing his news feeds by unfriending or unfollowing those who were using alcohol and drugs in unhealthy ways and posting pictures of themselves partying and/or high. Furthermore, Leo built up his mental muscles by holding himself back from logging on to social media when feeling low or sad. He did this by building up an arsenal of positive ways to combat depression, boredom, and feelings of FOMO and by learning to notice his most dangerous trigger, slides into upward social-comparison thinking, so he could stop the slide. For example, he upped his in-person communications by making a point to actually call his sponsor a minimum of five times per week, he made a weekly plan to have an in-person encounter with a friend, and he could usually count on writing in his journal to lift his mood too. By engaging in these activities Leo was developing both emotionally and intellectually!

Another way Leo minimized social media's negative effects on his recovery was by taking a well-planned break from social media altogether. He did this by setting a date for his break, deciding how long his break would last, and making sure to let his family and friends know about it in advance. Throughout his time off from social media, Leo made sure to keep in contact with friends and family via texting, FaceTime, and with old-fashioned phone calls.

But, as we know, nothing is either black or white, all good or all bad. This applies to social media. Over time, as Leo became more comfortable and secure in his recovery, he discovered the ways in which he could use social media to support his recovery, keep him connected socially, and even expand his social network. He did this by discovering accounts on Twitter, Instagram, and Facebook that were inspirational and motivated him to keep on track.

MENTAL WORKOUTS FOR CHANGING HABITS

Even though it's so difficult to change old habits and attitudes—like learning how to stop drinking alcohol, successfully cutting down on time spent on social media, or breaking unhealthy eating habits—it is not an impossible challenge. Our brain has the ability to change throughout our lifespan because of a process called *neuroplasticity*—or *brain plasticity*. This does not literally mean that our brains are made up of plastic but, rather, that just like plastic materials can bend and be reshaped, we can shape and remodel our brain's pathways with practice, time, and consistency.[7] This means that it is possible to replace old self-sabotaging patterns of thought and behavior with new healthy and rewarding ones when we help the brain reorganize itself by forming new connections between brain cells. All it takes is commitment, time, practice, and consistency. Just like our muscles develop and strengthen when we consistently train them, our brains do too.

SKILL-BUILDING STRATEGIES

Below are six mental workouts you can do every day to improve your emotional health.

- Exercise regularly, eat a balanced diet, and get enough rest. Physical health is closely connected to mental and emotional health. Regularly taking care of our bodies is a big step in achieving good mental and emotional health.
- Build positive experiences. It is important to become aware of the times you feel happy, satisfied, and accomplished and the situations in which good emotions are felt. Positive emotions come from positive experiences. Pursuing things we enjoy and being around people we like (virtually and in real life) releases *endorphins*, a chemical that makes us feel happy and good and rewires our brain to more easily and naturally do the things we enjoy rather than the things we don't derive pleasure from.
- Make your important relationships a daily priority. Humans are social creatures who crave the company of others. Having a strong social network significantly improves our emotional health and reduces our risk for depression and anxiety. Work on developing supportive and reciprocal relationships, both online and offline, with someone you can talk to regularly, who listens to you and supports you.
- Make time for contemplation and appreciation. On a daily basis, set aside a few minutes to think about the things you are grateful for in your life, such as friends, family, and good health.

- Build resilience and grit. Resilience and grit are intricately related to good emotional health. With practice and commitment, it's possible to build up your resiliency. One way to do this is to create a plan for when crises arise. Having a plan in place beforehand can help you stay focused and on track. Your plan can be as simple as having a list of support people to contact or a few coping behaviors you know work. Resilience and grit help us bounce back more quickly from life's inevitable setbacks and stops us from getting stuck in depression, anxiety, or other destructive mood states.
- Ask for help. Sometimes our own efforts to improve our circumstances or our emotional health are not effective. When this happens, getting professional help can make a big difference.

SOCIAL MEDIA, COGNITIVE DISTORTIONS, DEPRESSION, AND ANXIETY IN THE DIGITAL AGE

Nothing about living with depression and anxiety is easy. Multiple factors, many of which are beyond one's control, like genetics, hormones, and early environmental factors contribute to their manifestation. Social media has also been shown to trigger depression and anxiety as well as make their symptoms worse. But one very important variable we do have control over is our thought—what psychologists refer to as our *cognition*. It's also important to note that the thoughts that make up our cognitions are conscious, meaning we are aware of them. The good news is that this means we can immediately get to work on changing thoughts that lead us to feel negative emotions and to engage in harmful behaviors.

Think about this: Most of life happens between our ears—meaning, how we perceive and feel about our experiences, whether they're stressful, traumatic, sad, exciting, or joyful, comes from our inner thoughts, feelings, attitudes, and beliefs. But before we're able to attach feelings like joy, excitement, frustration, and anger to any given experience, we must first understand it by giving the experience a label or context. When our brain is in sync with reality, we correctly interpret our experiences, events, and social interactions and we can count on our emotions being accurate and healthy. But many people's brains regularly misread reality. Consequently, their inaccurate thoughts create what psychologists call *cognitive distortions*, causing a great deal of inner turmoil.

The idea that people are negatively affected by inaccurate interpretations of reality goes all the way back to the work of the early Greek stoic philosophers and is a central concept of cognitive behavioral therapy and dialectical behavioral therapy. As previously stated in chapter 3, cognitive distortions are simply ways that our mind convinces us of something that isn't really true. These inaccurate thoughts are used to reinforce negative thinking or emotions; "I can't do anything right" or "I'll never be in a relationship" are examples of cognitive distortions, for example. And when cognitive distortions spiral out of control, they exacerbate conditions like compare and despair, social comparison, envy, depression, and anxiety. Having distorted cognitions can also lead to unhealthy behaviors that only serve to worsen mood—like overspending because you feel as if "online it looks like everyone else has nicer things than me"; or maybe you isolate yourself because you "feel too ashamed to see people; everyone seems happier and more successful than me."

COGNITIVE DISTORTIONS AND SOCIAL MEDIA

Let's take a moment now to review three cognitive distortions commonly associated with social-media use.

1. Polarized thinking (black-and-white thinking). A person with polarized thinking categorizes people and situations as either/or, all/none, and good/bad. Cognitive distortions of this kind lead to emotional distress, because this kind of thinking doesn't take into account the complexity of most people and most situations. In addition, black-and-white thinking causes a person to experience life and feel emotions in extremes. Black-and-white thinking or all-or-none thinking is often what lurks underneath feelings of FOMO, envy, or low self-esteem triggered from social-media use. One way to avoid this pitfall while on social media is to learn how to be more flexible in your thinking and skillful at finding a middle ground. In short, finding the shades of gray between the

black and white. For example, if black-and-white thinking causes you to feel envious while scrolling through your friends' news-feeds or Instagram posts, remind yourself that life is complex and multilayered. This means that, in reality, no one's life can be perfect all the time. Make a list of at least three things you feel grateful for in your life and three positive qualities you love about yourself that you can refer to whenever you're feeling bad about yourself.

2. Jumping to conclusions. At the heart of this cognitive distortion is the belief that we know exactly what another person is feeling and thinking—and exactly why they act the way they do. It's a kin to being a mind reader. It's not hard to imagine how communicating via text, e-mail, and social-media messaging makes this kind of cognitive distortion more likely to manifest. This is because when important communication clues are missing, like body language and vocal tone, we're more likely to misunderstand what people are trying to communicate and therefore fill in the gaps by jump-ing to conclusions. Misunderstandings often lead to online dra-ma, disagreements, and conflict. One way to counteract this cog-nitive distortion is to simply ask yourself, "Do I have enough evidence to support my conclusion?"

3. Should statements. Many people use should statements like, "I should do this" or "I must do that" as a way to motivate them-selves. But did you know this kind of thinking often causes the opposite result? This is because should, ought, and must state-ments can cause us to feel angry, pressured, resentful, and de-pressed. For example, someone might feel they *should, ought,* or *must* get married because they're at an age where many of their friends are getting married, buying homes, having kids, and set-tling down. This person notices that after being on social media they question their direction in life. But in actuality, this person just completed graduate training in a field they love. Doing what they thought they should do, based on what their friends are doing, might have prevented them from pursuing their passions. And it's important to remember that what we say to ourselves influences how we feel!

SKILL-BUILDING STRATEGIES

Below are four ways you can challenge and change cognitive distortions when logged on and in real life.

- Keep a daily thought journal. The first step in making changes of any kind is to identify what exactly needs changing. Get in the habit of jotting down all the negative and troublesome thoughts you have when scrolling through social media. Extend this to include all the negative thoughts you have in real life as well.
- Make a habit of regularly examining your thoughts. Set aside a time each day to read over all the negative thoughts written down in your journal. When reviewing them, practice being as objective as possible. The purpose of this exercise is to learn to identify the most common cognitive distortions affecting your thinking and in what context or circumstances they are most likely to occur.
- Reflect, reflect, reflect. Get into the habit of closely examining your negative thoughts. For example, do you find that you often make negative generalizations? Or are you always jumping to conclusions about the lives of your friends on social media based on the pictures they post? And ask yourself, "Are my negative thoughts simply my personal opinions or hard-and-fast facts? Do I have actual evidence to back my thoughts? Is it possible for anyone to really know the ins and outs of the people's lives I have formed opinions about? When did I last see this person? Talk to this person?" Putting some emotional distance between your thoughts and emotions is key for cultivating the ability for self-reflection.
- Get outside of yourself. You can do this by simply asking yourself, "Would I think and feel the same way about a friend in the exact same situation?" All too often we are much harder on ourselves than we are with family and

friends. Learning to be loving and compassionate with ourselves is a huge step toward being able to diminish cognitive
distortions.

MEET OLIVIA, A SOCIAL-MEDIA USER WITH A BODY-IMAGE DISORDER

Olivia, an energetic and bubbly sophomore college student, came to see
me at her parents' urging. They were very concerned about their only
daughter's recent weight loss and preoccupation for all things fashion,
exercise, fitness, nutrition, and diet. At our first session Olivia told me,
"I was a normal-sized teenager. I might have had a little bit of baby fat
around my belly, but it didn't bother me much. It wasn't until college
that I became more focused on my appearance, weight, and body
shape. Now it's gotten to the point where it's pretty much all I think
about."

Eating disorders affect millions of Americans. In fact, it's estimated
that approximately thirty million Americans will suffer from an eating
disorder at some point in their lifetime. And although eating disorders
are the third most common chronic illness among adolescent girls, this
disease affects boys and men and women of all ages, races, religions,
and social and economic classes. [8]

Three main types of eating disorders have been identified.

1. Anorexia nervosa is characterized by weight loss often due to
   excessive dieting and exercise, sometimes to the point of starva-
   tion. People with anorexia feel they can never be thin enough and
   continue to see themselves as "fat" despite extreme weight loss.
2. Bulimia nervosa is marked by cycles of extreme overeating,
   known as *bingeing*, followed by purging or other behaviors to
   compensate for overeating. It is also associated with feelings of
   loss of control about eating.
3. Binge-eating disorder is characterized by regular episodes of extreme overeating and feelings of loss of control about eating.

BACK TO OLIVIA

"I don't ever want to gain back the fifteen pounds I've lost," Olivia told me one day in session.

> I know I'd feel so depressed if I did! The mere thought of it causes me to panic! But I do have to admit that I feel constantly stressed out about my diet and finding the time in my schedule to exercise while still having time to do my schoolwork.
>
> I try not to obsess about my appearance too much, and I know that being on social media can make my obsessions worse. When I'm on social media, I'm just constantly comparing myself to my friends and the social influencers I follow on Instagram or watch on You-Tube. I end up saying things like, "I should exercise more, I should do the exercises she's doing, or I must only eat raw foods. And then I'll look more like the girls I compare myself to."
>
> On the other hand, all the positive comments I get from my friends and followers from the pictures I post on my Snapchat, Instagram, and Twitter accounts—"You look so great" or "I wish I had your legs" and "Your abs are sick!"—make me feel great about myself, because I think, wow, other girls want to look like me. And then I become even more determined to be a certain body shape. I definitely do feel pressure from social media to look, act, and dress a certain way.

THE DANGERS OF SOCIAL-MEDIA USE AND BODY-IMAGE DISORDERS

Olivia recognized that her obsession with her weight, body shape, and appearance was unhealthy and that her social-media habits were reinforcing her destructive behaviors and beliefs. In fact, research studies are now showing social media's potential influence on the development and maintenance of eating and body-image disorders in the digital age.[9]

Think about this: social media's unique combination of factors including peer interactions, popularity of photo sharing, engagement in appearance comparisons with peers, and favorite "digital models" and the accessibility of mobile technology can dramatically increases the likelihood that young girls and women will internalize the "thin ideal," a concept linked to the development of eating and body-image disorders.[10]

The thin ideal is a sociocultural belief that an ideal female body *should be* slender, with a small waist and very little body fat. The act of *internalization* involves the integration of the thin ideal's attitudes, values, standards, and the opinions of others into one's own identity or sense of self. It's important to note that internalization is also a crucial component to the formation of the superego, the ethical component of the personality, made up of the moral standards by which the ego "individual" operates. The superego's criticisms, prohibitions, and inhibitions form a person's conscience, and its positive aspirations and ideals represent one's idealized self-image, or *ego ideal*. We can all observe the influence our superegos have on our behavior, emotions, and self-esteem through our inner voice, inner judge, or inner authority—and where many of our distorted *should*, *ought*, and *must* commands reside within our personalities. Millions of women and girls across the globe have incorporated the thin ideal into their superego and link it with positive life outcomes such as happiness, confidence, and sexual success.[11]

Olivia also revealed that social media provided her with an endless supply of peers and "models" to whom she could spend hours upon hours comparing herself. In chapter 3 I discussed Festinger's social-comparison theory, which purports that people naturally engage in social comparison with others in order to understand how and where they fit into the world when objective standards are not available.[12] Furthermore, adding fuel to the fire, findings from several studies indicate that most people, like Olivia, make upward comparisons around appearance and body image, contributing to what is now commonly referred to as a state of *compare and despair*.[13]

Think about this: When we open any number of social-media platforms and scroll through photos of vacations, celebrations with family and friends, and adorable pets, it's hard to not start thinking, "I'm not successful enough" and "I'm not good enough." Or even "I'm not thin enough or pretty enough." And when there's a constant stream of this kind of information, which influences how we think we should look, act, and feel, it's increasingly difficult to stave off feelings of inadequacy or inferiority—in order words, compare and despair. The slew of negative emotions driving a compare-and-despair state, like envy, resentment, and low-self-esteem, results in a great deal of emotional distress.

Getting stuck in a cycle of compare and despair ultimately prevents us from harnessing the power derived from fully accepting ourselves for who we are. Simply put, compare and despair robs us of appreciating our uniqueness and specialness. No two people in the whole wide world are exactly alike. Even identical twins! This means we are all unique and special in our own ways.

One way to prevent falling into the trap of compare and despair is to practice what's known as *radical acceptance*. Radical acceptance is a term associated with dialectical behavioral therapy, and it refers to the ability to accept our reality without judgment. It does not mean that we approve of events and situations that have happened or are happening but, rather, that we accept these circumstances, no matter how difficult they feel and are, as realities we might not be able to change at this very moment or ever. [14]

But it's not all bad news. The good news is, radical acceptance can lead to proactive behaviors, because acceptance helps us to direct our attention and focus on the steps we *can* take, in the realm of reality, to alleviate our emotional suffering. For example, by practicing radical acceptance, Olivia was able to let go of her unhealthy pursuit a "look" she'd never be able to achieve—along with 99 percent of all women and girls. Olivia was petite, and she had an athletic body shape, unlike the tall and long-limbed body shapes of typical models. It was unrealistic—not to mention potentially risky—for Olivia to push her body to meet the thin ideal. Radical acceptance also allowed Olivia to genuinely love herself for who she was versus who she wished she was.

MORE ON RADICAL ACCEPTANCE

At the heart of the technique and practice of radical acceptance is the ability to accept a difficult reality rather than fight against it. Research shows that we cause ourselves more emotional pain and suffering when we rail against situations and people that are beyond our control. But in reality, pain cannot be avoided; in fact our negative feelings are sometimes nature's way of telling us something is wrong.

It's important to note that radical acceptance does not support the notion that a difficult reality or relationship is okay and that one should just "give up" or "give in" to situations or relationships that are hurtful and destructive. Conversely, radical acceptance is acknowledging your reality so that you can marshal your psychological and emotional resources to move forward and heal.

The most meaningful lesson of radical acceptance is learning that life can be worth living even with its painful events. Accepting the things in our lives we can't change ultimately leads to more gratitude, peace, and contentment.

SKILL-BUILDING STRATEGIES

Below are four ways you can practice the skill of radical acceptance in your daily life.

- Identify the thoughts and behaviors that signal you're fighting against reality. For example, many people report noticing they feel angrier, bitter, and irritated when they catch themselves fighting against reality.
- Develop a balanced understanding of your reality. Too many times our emotions get in the way of our being able to skillfully and effectively interpret reality, causing us to distort things. Learning how to simply "report the facts" about upsetting events before taking action can help us implement effective ways to cope with difficult situations, therefore, saving ourselves from making difficult situations more difficult.
- Practice opposite action. Opposite action is an actual DBT skill set. List all the behaviors associated with actively accepting the facts of your reality. Then act as if you have already accepted the facts. For example, accepting the reality of a partner's deficits, such as the inability to be as emotionally supportive as you would like, might lead to you to be less critical of them and instead turn to friends or other

family members who can provide you with the support you need. Keep in mind no one person can meet another's every need.

- Practice everyday acceptance. This is another actual DBT skill. Too often we get caught up in the upsets of everyday hassles, inconveniences, and minor problems like traffic. Think of each of these situations as an opportunity to practice an attitude of acceptance. Getting into the habit of saying to yourself things like, "This is what life is like" and "Everyone feels this way at sometime or another" can make a *big* difference in coping with the ups and downs of life.

Source: Lane Pederson, *The DBT Deck for Clients and Therapists: 101 Mindful Practices to Manage Distress, Regulate Emotions & Build Better Relationships* (Eau Claire, WI: PESI Publishing, 2019).

HOW SOCIAL-MEDIA LITERACY HELPED OLIVIA

As I stated at the beginning of this chapter, key to being social-media literate is having critical-thinking skills. Gaining the skill set to evaluate media by examining what is pertinent and what content may be excluded, and accurately interpreting the overall message and purpose of a text, picture, or post makes us less vulnerable to being seduced into falling for misrepresentations and fabrications of reality—like when Instagram models post pictures of themselves that have been photoshopped, portraying unrealistic and unachievable standards of beauty, or news stories are run that aren't based on facts but, rather, serve only to instill fear and anxiety.

As for Olivia, her preoccupation with her diet, weight, and body shape was also being reinforced by her social-media consumption and habits. She would use social media for what she referred to as "inspiration for staying in shape and eating really healthy." Although her underlying drive and preoccupation for thinness is more complex and not simply caused by her social-media habits, raising Olivia's social-media literacy by examining why, when, and how she uses social media and learning how to decode visual messages and recognize images that have been photoshopped helped her gain a more realistic perspective of social media and use it in healthier and more adaptive and skillful ways.

After time, intention, and effort, Olivia was able to better regulate her goals for her own wellness and better see how social media could help or hinder her reaching those goals.

> Spending all my free time on social media, comparing myself to my friends, the social-media models I followed, and viewing fitness and diet profiles just reinforced the idea that felt I needed to look, act, and behave a certain way! I realize more and more how my social-media habits really did influence the way I felt about myself as a young woman. Being only nineteen, I'm still impressionable, and I'm learning I'm vulnerable to social messages that aren't healthy or even based in reality or that are only meant to sell an "image"—usually an unattainable one! Diet, fitness, and being healthy are important to me. But I can achieve this in a way that's realistic and positive.

By keeping a record of the sites she visited and the exact amount of time she spent logged on, Olivia was able to get an accurate picture of her digital footprint and the nature of the messages she was exposing herself to. While working on developing a healthier body image, Olivia agreed to take a break from social media. During this time Olivia and I focused on exploring her interests, passions, likes, and dislikes—the parts of her she felt she didn't know and that weren't tied to fitness, diet, and exercise. Over time, Olivia connected to her creative side, pursuing her interest in art by taking a drawing class. She also joined the gardening club at college! When Olivia was ready to return to spending time in digital spaces, she had an array of interests and passions to explore and learn about.

IN A NUTSHELL

Is your social-media use hurting you by causing you to feel more anxious, depressed, envious, and dissatisfied with your appearance and putting your recovery at risk? Take heart: you're not alone. There's no doubt that our exposure to digital content of any kind—whether it be Facebook, YouTube, Twitter, or Instagram—has the power to impact our mood and self-esteem and influences our perceptions of the world and those in it. In short, digital spaces influence our perspective, actions, attitudes, and behaviors. This happens whether we are conscious of it or not. Furthermore, the greater our emotional investment in social media, the more powerful it will be for us. For example, studies show that greater overall social-media use and high emotional investment in social media as a means for connection and validation were associated with insomnia and higher levels of anxiety, depression, and lower self-esteem. The direction of this relationship is still being debated, and the exact impact social media has on those struggling with a mental-health issue remains unclear.[15] For example, those higher in neuroticism may prefer to use social media as a means for meeting their needs for connection over connecting in person. And anxious and depressed individuals may use social media as a means for regulating emotions in much the same way a depressed or anxious individual might use alcohol, watching Netflix, or playing video games.

While the direction of the association between social-media use and eating disorders, depression, anxiety, substance abuse, and low self-esteem remains unclear, social-media literacy can help mitigate some of the risks associated with social media's impact on these disorders by helping users learn to use social media in skillful and effective ways. Following are some recommendations to help you become more literate in your social-media use in order to improve your screen health.

RECOMMENDATIONS

1. Examine your use of cognitive distortion when logged on. Do you jump to conclusions or generalize about someone's existence based their newsfeeds, pictures, and posts? Do you compare yourself to others online and across all domains such as attractiveness, success, or wealth? Although social media does give some facts and information about another's life, it cannot show the nuances and details that truly represent the complexities of all our existence.

2. Prioritize learning the ins and outs of social-media literacy. The digital world can be a space of incredible resources and learning opportunities, but it also opens us to the challenges of its intended and unintentional effects on our emotional well-being. Keep up-to-date regarding technology's ability to alter reality—for example, the availability of certain filters and photoshopping

capacities—so that you're able to identify what's real versus what has been digitally altered.

3. Learn to think critically. In our media-saturated culture, it's hard to escape the onslaught of messages about how we should look, act, and behave. Learn to identify and think critically about untrue and unhealthy media messages. For example, get into the habit of asking yourself, "What words or images got my attention? What is the purpose of this particular message?" If models or celebrities are featured, ask yourself, "Were they airbrushed or photoshopped, and were filters used to achieve their look? Does anyone really look like that? What values, beliefs and lifestyles are being communicated in this post? Are theses messages in line with my truest beliefs and values?"

5

BREAKING UP IN THE DIGITAL AGE

The human psyche, like human bones, is strongly inclined towards self-healing.

—John Bowlby[1]

Breaking up is difficult, and in a 24-7 social-media-driven world that values constant connection, mourning the end of a relationship is more complicated than ever.

Whether your breakup is with a romantic partner or a family member, and regardless of who initiated it, ending a relationship is an emotionally arduous process. Progressing through the stages of mourning and seeking emotional acceptance and closure after a breakup requires time, patience, self-love, and letting go of old feelings. There is no question that social media and your digital presence can play a critical role in how you adapt to your new reality. Examining and adjusting your social-media practices will have a real and profound effect on your recovery.

In my practice, discussing my clients' social-media habits has become an important part of treatment. Sites like Facebook and Instagram have a significant impact on our lives and relationships and, in turn, on our psychological well-being.

Do you need to go on a "digital detox diet" in order to give yourself the space to heal after a breakup? Not necessarily. You do, however, need to take some time to examine how and why you use social media, because even small changes in your social-media habits can make a big difference in how you feel. In this chapter, you'll meet Megan, a young woman struggling with accepting a fresh breakup, and Seth, a guy in his fifties coming to terms with his "breakup" from his alcoholic father. Regardless of the circumstances surrounding your loss, this chapter will help you understand why you are experiencing certain feelings and what actions you can take to care for yourself.

MOURNING IS MESSY

You have probably heard that grieving is a process, or that there are several stages to grieving. Thanks to the pioneering research of Swiss-American psychiatrist Elisabeth Kübler-Ross, we know this to be true. Kübler-Ross studied death and dying in the late 1960s and determined that grieving is a process following five unique stages: denial, anger, bargaining, depression, and acceptance. When we experience a loss, including the loss of a relationship, we process our feelings in these sequential steps.[2]

Mourning is rarely a neat process; it's messy at best. When mourning a loss, it's important to keep in mind that our ultimate goal is the stage of acceptance. Acceptance brings about feelings of peace and under-standing, which are necessary for fully appreciating the reality that loss is a part of living. Acceptance also gives us courage to let go of past relationships that no longer serve us, creating room for new and healthy relationships.

Yet in the age of social media, as long as both you and your former partner have a digital presence, finding acceptance and closure is ques-tionable, as a digital connection will always be available. The ease with which we can access photos and details of an ex-partner's personal life makes it hard to resist doing just that when the desire bubbles up inside of us. As you will discover, however, indulging these urges comes at a hefty emotional cost.

UNPACKING COMPLICATED MOURNING

Social media allows us the benefit of distracting ourselves as soon as we feel an uncomfortable emotion. The avoidance of painful emotions is normal, but it's important to note that by denying ourselves the opportunity to deal with "messy" emotions like sadness, loneliness, or anxiety, we're setting ourselves up for failure. Exacerbated by social media, normal mourning can quickly escalate to complicated mourning.

What is the difference between normal mourning and complicated mourning? A person experiencing normal mourning maintains their self-esteem and the hope that things will get better during the mourning process. A person coping with complicated mourning is consumed by feelings of despair and hopelessness. Complicated mourning can manifest itself physically, through insomnia, weight changes, panic attacks, and substance abuse. It can prevent sufferers from attending school or work or from fulfilling daily responsibilities. In a word, complicated mourning is all-consuming. [3]

Turning to social media in the midst of mourning—particularly when mourning the end of a relationship—only increases the chance that it will progress to complicated mourning. Instead of looking for an online escape when you feel sad or lonely, try self-soothing methods to cope with your feelings.

Self-soothing methods are behaviors that are meant to relax us and calm our senses. Some common examples include meditation, reading, listening to music, watching television, taking a warm bath, exercising, or calling a friend to talk. The goal of self-soothing is to channel your negative, sad, or otherwise uncomfortable feelings into either neutral or positive ones by focusing your attention on something else.

SKILL-BUILDING STRATEGY

It's important to learn ways to calm down intense emotions, like anger, frustration, anxiety, and sadness, especially while in the throes of mourning a loss. Below are four tips to help get you started.

- Write down at least five to seven self-soothing methods that you'd like to try.
- Practice one per day for one week.
- After one week, take time to consider which activities made you feel better.

- Commit to working self-soothing care practices into your daily routine.

MOURNING A RELATIONSHIP VERSUS MOURNING A DEATH

It's not uncommon to hear comparisons between the end of a relationship and the death of a loved one. Many people equate breaking up to the loss of a loved one—whether the breakup is between romantic partners, friends, siblings, or parents and children. While it's true that both breakups and deaths require time to mourn, there are several stark differences between the two.

When someone we love dies, we need to figure out how to preserve a relationship with them even though they are no longer physically present. When I was thirty-six years old, my father died from what doctors suspected was a massive stroke or heart attack. I was completely devastated by his sudden death. My reality had unmistakably changed, and there was nothing I could do to reverse that change. I simply had to learn to accept my father's passing and live life in the face of loss.

After the death of a loved one, we still remain emotionally attached to this person, even though they are not physically with us. Learning to remain attached when someone we love dies requires us to form an internalized, symbolic attachment. They stay with us by always being in our minds and hearts. It's been seventeen years since my father died, and I still regularly share memories of him with my two adult daughters, my husband, and my close friends. I don't want to forget my father or replace the important role he had in my life.

On the other hand, when we mourn the loss of a relationship, much of the work that must be done to achieve acceptance actually requires that we forget. This doesn't mean literally forgetting an ex-partner and wiping all traces of them from your memory. Rather, through a process known as *detachment*, moving on requires us to emotionally detach from that person in order to "make room" for new relationships and attachments.

Healthy detachment from a past relationship lays the groundwork for letting go, moving on, and loving again. This process can only happen after consciously relinquishing and working through the feelings—

both positive and loving as well as negative and angry—that we harbor toward the person we are no longer in a relationship with. This type of emotional honesty can be challenging, but it is a major component of healthy grieving. Without emotional detachment, there can be no acceptance of loss.

Talking about your feelings helps. Talking is healing. When we express pent-up feelings, we experience a genuine sense of release, which is both cathartic and clarifying. Throughout the mourning process, talk honestly about your feelings and emotions with a trusted friend, family member, or mental-health professional. Having a trusted person to talk with about difficult feelings related to loss decreases the chances of using repression or other self-destructive defense mechanisms. Lots of people hesitate to talk about their feelings because they believe doing so is a sign of emotional weakness. Others don't open up because they're afraid to express their true selves. And for some, it can be hard to identify emotions. Although talking about feelings is difficult, its many benefits far outweigh any potential embarrassment.

SKILL-BUILDING STRATEGY

It's normal to feel stressed out and depressed when dealing with life's challenges, like breaking up with a partner, losing a job, or grieving a death. But keeping our feelings pent-up can be emotionally overwhelming. When we allow ourselves to talk about challenges and feelings, we release some of that tension and stress.
Here's how talking can help.

- We gain new perspectives. Talking about our feelings and problems allows us to hear our own thoughts. Solutions often naturally occur to us; but if they don't, friends, family, or a therapist can make helpful suggestions.
- Talking deepens intimacy. Sharing the ups and downs of life with others strengthens our emotional ties and gives us the feeling of belonging that we need to emotionally thrive. Having close friends enriches our lives and decreases our risks for depression, anxiety, and loneliness.

- We develop "self-talk" skills. Talking to ourselves can help with changing the way we think and act. Self-talk works by erasing our counterproductive thoughts and replacing them with positive and productive ones. Develop self-talk skills by making a list of your negative thoughts and then creating a series of positive statements to counteract those negative beliefs.

THE DETACHMENT/SOCIAL-MEDIA CONUNDRUM

While detachment is a critical piece of mourning and moving on from a former relationship, it is not always easy to achieve when social media is readily available to us at any time and in any place. Social media's availability makes it hard to not indulge our natural curiosity to "take a quick peek" at what an ex-partner might be up to these days, causing fresh reminders of the loss and making it harder to grieve. According to the American Psychological Association's annual stress report from 2017, Americans who constantly check their e-mail, texts, and social-media accounts are more likely to have higher stress levels. This tendency is referred to as *constant checking*.[4] In regards to mourning a loss, constant checking prevents us from gaining the emotional space we need to properly grieve and heal. Constant checkers, unbeknownst to them, actually put themselves at risk for developing digital self-sabotaging behaviors.

MEET MEGAN, A CONSTANT SOCIAL-MEDIA CHECKER

Megan is an attractive and intelligent young woman in her early twenties, fresh out of college and beginning her professional career. She came to me for help dealing with feelings of loss after the sudden breakup of her long-term relationship with her high school boyfriend, Scott.

Despite attending different universities, Megan and Scott had relied on technology and social media to sustain a five-year relationship. It was a shock to Megan when Scott abruptly broke off their relationship after meeting someone during their senior year of college. Megan felt completely blindsided. After their breakup, the two remained friends on social media, and Megan found herself in the habit of compulsively checking in on Scott's life and his new relationship.

As a result, Megan was depressed and having difficulty concentrating on tasks at her new job. She was also having trouble eating and sleeping, and she was drinking alcohol more frequently than usual. Her constant checking was not only causing her to feel more stressed, it was also interfering with her ability to properly grieve.

Sound familiar? Megan's experience is a common one. A recent survey conducted by the American Psychological Association found that more than eight out of ten Americans are attached to their gadgets. Of those surveyed, 86 percent say they constantly or often check their e-mails, texts, and social-media accounts. People who constantly check their gadgets are more stressed and anxious than those who do not use technology and social media as frequently, and this added stress compounds mourning.[5]

This connection to technology denies us the time to mourn and detach from our romantic relationships. When we do not allow ourselves this time, major losses—like the end of a relationship—will snowball into more serious problems, preventing us from living the fulfilling life we envision for ourselves. In order to properly mourn a loss, we must allow ourselves physical and digital space from former partners.

Constant checking isn't the only thing that can inhibit the mourning process. Studies show that consuming social media passively—ingesting content by scrolling through news, public posts, broadcasts, and public profiles without interacting with them—is linked to negative well-being. Passive consumption of social media increases feelings of depression and loneliness. It can also exacerbate feelings of envy and fear of missing out, all of which can damage our self-esteem.[6] Feeling more sad and anxious when mourning a loss is the last thing to which we should be voluntarily subjecting ourselves.

In response to Megan's constant checking and passive social-media consumption, in session she and I discussed the idea of taking scheduled breaks from social media throughout the day. At first, she was nervous about the idea and expressed concern that it might make her more anxious and lonely. Megan also knew she'd be left wondering what Scott was doing and was worried about where her imagination might take her.

I explained to Megan that taking conscious and planned breaks from social media is a form of self-care. The break doesn't have to be forever; in fact, even a small break can be impactful. Any social-media hiatus, whether it be for an hour or—if you're feeling ambitious—a whole day, is time well spent healing from your loss.

Taking breaks from social media also helps dissipate strong negative emotions. It is when we're in emotionally charged spaces that we're more likely to use social media in hurtful ways or to engage in any number of self-destructive behaviors that hinder our recovery, like drinking too much, overspending, or overeating. Instead, consider the following exercise.

SKILL-BUILDING STRATEGIES

Write your feelings down. Ask yourself,

- What would happen if you decided not to go on social media when missing an ex-partner?
- What's the worst thing that can happen if you do not check an ex-partner's social media?
- Is there something else you can do instead of going on social media, such as taking a walk or calling a friend or family member?

THE SELF-SABOTAGING CYCLE OF CONSTANT CHECKERS

Constant checking, like the habit that Megan was indulging in, reflects curiosity. Curiosity is a normal and necessary part of the human condition. It sparks creativity and learning, and it makes our lives exciting. Sometimes, however, our primal drive to be curious can lead to perilous and self-sabotaging decisions.

When Megan and I examined her social-media use, she painted a clear picture of her self-sabotaging habits: A great deal of her time was spent frequently and passively scrolling through Scott's social-media accounts, watching videos or reading posts intended for his friends on-line, and repeatedly visiting his updates, pictures, and profile information. After Megan emerged from one of her social media "binges," as she referred to this behavior, she reported feeling worse than she had just moments before. This behavior created a new set of problems for Megan. Not only was she feeling sad about her lost relationship, she was now also feeling bad about the time she had lost and her inability to care for herself in a positive way that would move her forward in life.

She was in need of an aha moment.

Aha moments can be life-changing, revealing emotions and thoughts that were previously unconscious or hidden from us. Feelings and thoughts that were once deeply buried become conscious and illuminated, and our feeling of powerlessness to change our behaviors and thoughts begins to recede. This insight allows us the ability to approach and solve our problems with a skill set comprised of conscious, rational, and moral decision-making abilities.

Megan's aha moment was realizing that she turned to Scott's social media when certain thoughts bubbled up inside her: She was using social media as an escape. Instead of working to accomplish her own goals and daily responsibilities, she was preoccupied with feelings of longing, concerns about her drinking, and frustration with the time she had spent devoted to constant checking. Her habits were interfering with her ability to carve out the emotional space she needed in order to process her feelings and to focus on her own life postbreakup.

Megan's behaviors illustrate the pull of self-sabotaging behaviors, how hard it is to let go of deep attachments, and how social media not only prolongs grief but also complicates the emotional work of detaching and downgrading old attachments.

Every time you log on to social media, it stunts your mourning process and personal growth. One of Megan's goals in treatment was to change how she related to others in real life as well as online. Gaining insight into your self-sabotaging behaviors is a significant step in helping yourself and ultimately in being able to make lasting lifestyle changes. After all, we can't fix self-sabotaging social-media habits if we are not conscious of what's underneath them.

One way to reduce self-sabotaging cycles of constant checking is by making a point to stay connected to friends and family while mourning your breakup. Making an effort to see friends and family has been shown to reduce self-sabotaging behaviors and to decrease FOMO, anxiety, and depression. Paying attention to the ways in which you interact online, what you share, and the quality of your virtual relationships is also important, as they have a real impact on your life and mental health.

STOP THE CYCLE OF SELF-SABOTAGE

If you often find that, despite good intentions, your efforts are often backfiring, you may be unknowingly using self-sabotaging tactics and engaging in self-sabotaging behaviors.

Self-sabotaging behaviors are made up of a complex set of actions and thoughts that ruin our good intentions and negatively affect our relationships, employment, health, quality of life, and emotional well-being. These self-sabotaging behaviors are usually learned in childhood through example and by modeling, and it is not uncommon for these behaviors to be passed down from one generation to the next.

It's important to understand that since self-sabotaging behaviors are initially reinforced, in the short-term they allow temporary relief from feelings of anxiety and stress by means of avoidance, but in the long-term they lead to chronic depression, low self-esteem, substance abuse, poor interpersonal relationships, life goals not actualized, and stifled potential.

Following are some examples of self-sabotaging behaviors and thoughts.

- Agreeing to commitments and tasks that you'd like to say no to
- Procrastinating
- Neglecting your physical health (e.g., a poor diet, lack of exercise, abusing alcohol)
- Frequently lying to people in order to avoid a conflict
- Being impulsive with actions and feelings
- Believing and needing to always be right
- Not finishing projects or tasks you've started
- Focusing only on the negative aspects of your life or yourself

SKILL-BUILDING STRATEGIES

Although self-sabotaging behaviors can be difficult to let go of, it is not impossible. Instead, replace self-sabotaging behaviors with helpful, positive behaviors and thoughts. Below are a few strategies to help you get out of the self-sabotage trap.

- Acknowledge that you engage in self-sabotaging behaviors and thoughts. The first step in addressing any issue is to acknowledge it. Acknowledging our struggles allows us to take personal responsibility for them and makes us aware that it is within our power to make real and lasting changes in our life.
- Identify when you most often use self-sabotaging tactics. Write down specific situations where you recognize you use self-defeating thoughts and behaviors. Identify the feelings you're avoiding by using self-sabotaging tactics, such as anxiety, fear of hurting someone else's feelings, or avoiding a conflict.
- Have a plan for challenging times. Take the time to brainstorm with a trusted friend, family member, or a mental-health professional in order to find alternative ways of responding to future challenging situations. It's difficult for most people to think clearly when they are feeling anxious or stressed. Being prepared with healthy tactics when facing a challenging situation improves your chances for making changes.
- Seek professional help. Self-sabotage behaviors are complex, and being able to actually change them may require the help of a professional. Together, exploring the underlying causes of your self-destructive behaviors can bring about the insights you need to make lasting changes.

BREAKING UP WITH FAMILY

We rely on our family members to keep us safe physically and emotionally, to love us unconditionally, and to support and encourage us. So when our family members fail us, it can leave a deep wound. Family ties are usually broken due to a myriad of dysfunctional dynamics, including addiction, neglect, and emotional, physical, or sexual abuse. Sometimes one or more of these abuses or neglects are present together.

Such is the case with Seth, a fifty-one-year-old patient of mine.

Seth is a father of three, happily married for twenty-two years when he initially came to see me to learn to manage his anger and frustration. Recently, he'd had an angry outburst at work that was so severe it negatively impacted his performance review, and he was concerned about losing his job. Over the course of therapy, Seth revealed that he hadn't spoken to his father in over three years. His father's alcoholism and emotional abuse had led to Seth's decision to cut ties.

When Seth was six months into treatment, he told me that his father's Facebook profile appeared as a suggested friend. For Seth, this triggered anger that he had long suppressed.

Once Seth had discovered this important trigger, he and I were able to work together to come up with a series of strategies to reduce the toll those triggers took on him and sometimes remove the triggers altogether.

Knowing how to properly identify and neutralize triggers is an important part of social-media engagement. Following are some tips that can help you avoid self-destructive media habits.

SKILL-BUILDING STRATEGIES

Identify triggers that lead to self-destructive social-media habits. *Triggers* are people, places, and things that remind us of a past trauma or upsetting event. Triggers can cause us to feel overwhelming sadness, anxiety, or panic. As for social media, it's important that we gain an understanding of our particular triggers so we can put a plan in place to avoid exposing ourselves to content that will cause us pain. Below are a few suggestions to help.

- "Friend" people you either know or want to get to know because you share similar interests. Having a good sense of who is most likely going to pop up on your news feed naturally diminishes triggers.
- Stick with only one or two social-media platforms. Keeping up with multiple social-media platforms is not only anxiety producing, it's also time-consuming. And not having the time to complete important tasks only adds to our anxiety and depression.
- Check in with yourself before logging on. If you're in the middle of a bout with anxiety or depression, take a break from social media. Step back for as long as is needed. You can spend your time doing other activities, like going for a walk, seeing a friend, or reading a book.
- Have a plan in place for coping with any feelings that emerge should you be reminded of photos, memories, or other milestones with an ex-partner or family member. Try one of the self-soothing methods we discussed earlier, and, once again, take a social-media break until the end of the day or holiday to avoid feeling further triggered.

Living with family estrangement in the digital age presents its own set of unique challenges. Before the ubiquity of social media, family estrangement often meant a clean break. Today social media makes it almost impossible to avoid mentions, photos, or updates of an estranged family member. These momentary peeks into their world can be painful reminders of what we are missing out on.

Although well-intentioned, features like Facebook's Memories feature or its birthday, anniversary, and "friendship anniversary" reminders are common triggers for people dealing with estranged family members. Several months into his therapy, Seth began to talk more openly and honestly with me about his social-media habits, revealing that the birthday, holiday, and "friendship anniversary" reminders and videos that had been curated for him had begun to negatively affect him and brought up feelings of anger, hurt, and shame. These feelings would linger for days, Seth told me, and affect his relationships with family and close friends, his sleep patterns, his appetite, and his patience.

Feelings like the ones Seth experienced when he was reminded of his father don't shake off easily; they can linger for hours or days.

Be mindful of when you decide to go on social media, too. If you're facing a stressful day or know it's the birthday or anniversary of someone with whom you no longer have a relationship, avoid using social-media outlets that might remind you of this relationship. This will save you some heartache. Seth and I worked diligently over the next year to identify and predict the times in his life that would be especially hard for him. He made sure to curtail his social-media consumption during these times. He learned to center his social-media usage around his most important relationships, like with his children, wife, sister, and close friends.

Seth also found ways to enhance his social-media experience by being more intentional in his interactions. Studies investigating the power of social media suggest that tailored, specific, and targeted communications have positive outcomes on our well-being.[7] This means interactions with friends or family members with whom we are already close offline, and not with a person or virtual "friend" with whom we are not as emotionally connected. Just as is the case in our offline lives, our more-established and -intimate relationships have a positive effect on our well-being and provide us with emotional support during our most challenging times.

PERSONAL GROWTH

Everything we do, including using social media, impacts our well-being. Some activities leave us feeling nurtured, lifted, energized, and hopeful, while others leave us feeling discouraged, sad, emotionally exhausted, and physically drained. Not all social-media consumption is inherently bad. Many people feel that technology and social media have improved their lives. The goal of this book is to help strike a healthy balance between our virtual lives and our real-time lives.

While there's no perfect way to deal with loss, following are some recommendations to help minimize the pitfalls of social-media consumption during the mourning process and help you gain closure. Although these recommendations may seem like obvious advice, working through mourning and grief requires connecting emotional knowledge with common sense in order to achieve the final, peaceful stage of grieving: acceptance.

RECOMMENDATIONS

1. Take a one-day hiatus from social media. Not seeing an ex-partner's activity on social media allows for healing to take place. After your break, ask yourself the following questions: What was the hardest part about taking a break from social media? How did you feel afterward? Consider extending your break or setting limits with yourself until you feel logging on to social media and seeing your ex-partner doesn't negatively impact your recovery.

2. Create a safe space on social media. Consider other options for virtual connection, such as starting a new group text, Twitter List, or a Facebook group that includes only your closest friends. These options allow you to limit the activity and users you follow online and can help minimize FOMO. Targeted and specific communications from close friends, our strong ties, have the most positive impact on us.

3. Identify triggers that lead to self-destructive social-media habits. Should you be reminded of photos, memories, or other milestones with an ex-partner or family members, it is important to have a plan in place for coping with these feelings. Try a self-soothing method we discussed earlier, and take a social-media break until the end of the day or holiday to avoid feeling triggered further.

4. Remain hopeful. There's no doubt that mourning a breakup is hard work, but you won't feel this way forever. It can be both physically and emotionally exhausting, so knowing we ought to be more tender and compassionate with ourselves is helpful. Make a concerted effort to utilize self-soothing methods, and turn to a mental-health professional for support if you need it.

6

MEDICATING WITH TECHNOLOGY

There are two ways of spreading light; to be the candle or the mirror that reflects it.

—Edith Wharton[1]

Did you know that the average American spends ten hours and nine minutes glued to screens daily?[2] This chapter asks questions such as, "How many hours daily do I spend interacting with my gadgets without realizing how much time has passed?" and "What was I expecting when I posted that picture, made that comment, tweeted that thought, or sent that text?" Together we will explore how the underlying drive to avoid negative emotions, such as boredom, anger, and anxiety, drives unhealthy social-media use and contributes to Internet addiction. We will also learn how obsessively checking social media, e-mails, texts, and other virtual sites robs us of valuable time that could be used for personal development—time we can never get back.

By examining psychological concepts such as mentalizing, emotional intelligence, self-awareness, and how feeling bad can sometimes be good for you, you'll discover ways to improve screen health. But first, take a moment to reflect on your social-media habits.

TEST YOURSELF USING THE SOCIAL MEDIA DISORDER SCALE

If you suspect your social-media use is holding you back from living a happier, healthier, more fulfilling, productive life, it's probably time to take a deeper look into your social-media habits. By rating yourself using the Social Media Disorder Scale, a nine-question survey below, you'll be able to see how your social-media consumption might be negatively affecting your life.[3] This nine-question survey is designed to distinguish between healthy and unhealthy social-media use and measure dimensions of preoccupation, tolerance, withdrawal, persistence, displacement, interpersonal problems, deception, escape, and conflict.

Simply answer yes or no to each of the nine questions below.

During the past year, have you . . .

> . . . regularly found that you can't think of anything else but the moment that you will be able to use social media again?
> . . . regularly felt dissatisfied because you wanted to spend more time on social media?
> . . . often felt bad when you could not use social media?
> . . . tried to spend less time on social media but failed?
> . . . regularly neglected other activities (e.g., hobbies, sport) because you wanted to use social media?
> . . . regularly had arguments with others because of your social-media use?
> . . . regularly lied to your parents or friends about the amount of time you spend on social media?
> . . . often used social media to escape from negative feelings?
> . . . had serious conflict with your parents, brother(s), or sister(s) because of your social-media use?

If you answered yes to five or more of these questions, you are probably using social media in unhealthy ways. Remember, while there is no formal social-media disorder diagnosis, breaking problematic social-media use can be addressed with a mental-health professional so those using social media unhealthily can learn to maintain social relationships in a healthy way both on- and offline.

To illustrate what disordered social-media use could look like, let's now meet Al, an older man who is struggling—but eventually succeeds—at getting his disordered social-media use under control.

Al, a sixty-three-year-old married and successful business owner, came to therapy at his wife's insistence: They were on the verge of divorce. Al's wife was going to leave him if he didn't do something about his constant computer use or what his wife referred to as his "computer addiction."

They had two adult children and a new grandson. Al's wife was feeling completely and utterly emotionally neglected by him, so much so that she often told him, "I feel like a widow!" Whenever Al wasn't working and had free time, he'd choose to spend it glued to his iPad, on Twitter or Facebook, playing games, reading the news, or watching pornography for hours and hours.

When I first met with Al, I asked him directly, "Do you have any idea why you prefer to be on your computer instead of spending time with your wife?"

"It's not that I don't want to spend time with my wife," Al responded flatly.

> Rather, I'm just bored. Bored with life. All I do is go to work, eat dinner, go on my computer, and go to sleep. Then I wake up the next day and do the exact same thing, day after day after day. I don't want to go out to lunch or go to a yoga class—the things my wife would like me to do with her. To be honest, being on my computer relaxes me. It takes me to a different place, where I don't have to think about my problems about work, my kids, or my wife.

I hear this a lot in my practice: "I eat because I'm bored." "I drink because I'm bored." "I gamble because I'm bored." "I'm having an affair because I'm bored." "I overexercise because I'm bored." "I watch pornography because I'm bored."

As I got to know Al, he shared with me that his parents had had a tumultuous relationship. They'd often fought about trivial matters and would yell and scream at each other for hours on end. Sometimes their arguments would last for days. As a child, Al would escape and isolate in his bedroom, where he felt both safe and in control, reading science fiction. He especially loved reading superhero comic books. He often fantasized that he was one of the superheroes he would read about to avoid feeling frustrated, anxious, helpless, or depressed. Furthermore, when Al was a senior in college, his mother was diagnosed with cancer.

And his emotional escapes of daydreaming, fantasizing, and isolating ramped up to the point where he wouldn't come out of his room, except to eat dinner, until the next morning.

Unfortunately, Al's mother didn't live to see him graduate from college and business school, get married, or have his first child. And his mother's death left a deep hole in Al's psyche, even though he'd had ambivalent feelings toward his mother.

After turning sixty, Al noticed he was feeling depressed and that he was focusing on his mortality more than usual. But he felt able to keep his depression at bay with his new hobby: scrolling through Twitter and Facebook, playing games, reading the news, and looking at pornography. However, immediately after his grandson was born, Al's feelings of depression intensified. And once again, his emotional escapes ramped up to the point where he wasn't leaving his bedroom except to join his wife for dinner or, when his wife insisted, for an occasional walk. Al finally agreed with his wife: he needed to talk to someone, because he feared his social-media and tech habits would destroy his marriage, and then he'd lose his family.

Over the course of therapy, Al became aware of the fact that he hadn't fully mourned the loss of his mother and that he hadn't been aware of the powerlessness he'd felt as a child. His computer use, in the short term, numbed the emotional pain he felt when his mind drifted back to the past. Al was also aware that he wasn't able to live in the present moment or to feel optimistic about his future. In other words, Al was stuck in his grief! Just like he was stuck glued to his computer screen.

"Being on social media, playing games, interacting on Twitter, and, I'm ashamed to admit, looking at pornography was a way for me to avoid the pain and powerlessness I still felt about my mother's death. Feeling bored—like my life was lacking in life—was really my detaching from my deep feelings of grief and loss."

In treatment, Al worked through his grief and mourning and displaced feelings of powerlessness. This helped him be more present and embrace his life. Eventually, Al was able to once again enjoy being a husband, father, and, now, grandfather.

WHAT'S UNHEALTHY SOCIAL-MEDIA USE?

Although there is no such thing as an *official* diagnosis of computer addiction, there's lots of compelling research telling us that nonetheless the addiction is real. The term *addiction* refers to a complex condition that is manifested by compulsive behaviors to use substances or engage in harmful and risky behaviors like sex, pornography, shopping, and eating despite their harmful consequences. Just like those who suffer from other addictions like substance or alcohol abuse, people struggling with compulsive computer use tend to isolate themselves from friends and family and lie about their computer use and the sites they visit and are unable to stop their computer use despite attempts to lessen their frequency or quit. In a nutshell, in place of using drugs and alcohol, for example, to make them selves feel better, people who suffer from compulsive computer usage derive feelings of joy, happiness, and euphoria from their digital consumption, as one would with another type of addiction. Those who suffer from computer addiction tend to prioritize computer use above all other daily activities and responsibilities. A computer addiction, as with any other type of addiction, can lead to serious life problems, such as issues with careers, relationships, and health, resulting from an excessive amount of time on the computer and neglecting important obligations.[4]

SELF-MEDICATING WITH TECH

When we're bored we feel sluggish, uninspired, weary or apathy. Boredom is emotionally painful. I get it. And like most people, I don't like feeling bored either so I can appreciate the desire to want to escape it. But, more times than not, chronic boredom, such as the type Al was experiencing, isn't just a benign and normal state of being but rather it's a symptom of a much deeper issue like unresolved anger and rage, powerlessness, depression, grief, anxiety or feelings around lacking purpose and meaning in one's life.

Self-medicating negative emotions, like boredom, is not a new phenomenon. The term *self-medicating* was originally associated with alcohol or substance abuse. Anything we do to suppress, deny, avoid, or minimize negative emotions is considered a self-medicating behavior.

Al was using the computer to self-medicate his repressed feelings of helplessness and powerlessness regarding his mother's sickness and his feelings about losing her at such a young and tender age. Al needed help mourning the loss of his mother, which he'd never done before.

I want to point out that a serious consequence of self-medicating behaviors is their tendency to cause us more problems than the original problem we were self-medicating in the first place. For example, it's not hard to see how self-medicating behaviors like watching hours of pornography online would create conflict in our relationships, how overshopping and overspending could land us in debt, how overeating to the point of overweight can become a serious medical issue, and how overexercising can cause physical injuries.

Generally speaking, we all have had moments when we feel "stuck" or like we've hit a wall. And, as it was for Al, being stuck is an inner feeling of stagnation and paralysis that can feel beyond our control. When we feel stuck—whether it's because we never grieved a significant loss or we feel stuck in a relationship or in a job because we're afraid of change—it's normal that we begin to question our core purpose, our life's path, and even our ability to make decisions. Being stuck causes us to feel hopeless and uninspired, and it's not a surprise to learn that feeling stuck can feel like boredom, leading to self-medicating behaviors like overdrinking, overeating, overshopping, spending too much time on social media, and overgambling, for example.

So you might now ask, "What are some of the other common causes that lead us to feeling stuck?" Some of the most common causes include the following.

- Underlying depression
- Self-doubt
- Fear of making mistakes
- Feeling powerless and hopeless
- Ambivalence
- Discomfort with trying new things and getting out of your comfort zone
- No longer feeling curious to try new things

Although these are common feelings that everyone can experience, it's important to remind ourselves that all change begins within us and that we are our own agents of change.

SKILL-BUILDING STRATEGY

Below are five things you can do now to help you get "unstuck" and move forward.

- Every day, do at least one thing you enjoy. Whatever that is—whether reading, working out, or just sitting and relaxing—make it a priority as much as your other responsibilities, like working, paying the bills, and taking care of family. Doing the things we love brings new and positive energy into our lives. And the more we do it, the more natural it will become.
- It's okay to feel stuck. This may sound counterintuitive, but it's not. Sometimes the more we resist an emotion or thought, the stronger it becomes. Feeling stuck from time to time is normal. Instead of thinking it is wrong or bad to feel stuck, allow yourself to be present in this emotion so your mental energy can go toward figuring out what changes need to be made to move forward, rather than focusing your energy on self-criticism about feeling stuck in the first place.
- Do something outside of your comfort zone. Living life only within our comfort zone inhibits us from growing in countless ways. Figure out what you'd like to try but have been hesitant to act on because of fear or self-doubt. Make a conscious effort to become aware of what gives you a deep sense of joy and excitement.

MEET MELODY

Melody couldn't stop posting selfies throughout her day. In fact, much of her time was spent around planning for, traveling for, primping for, prepping for, and posting her selfies and then assessing how well-received or not her posts were. Melody was also compulsively trying to outdo whatever her last post was. So garnering more likes and more comments than whatever her most recent post had generated became her ultimate goal. Melody said to me in a session one day, early in our work together, "Posting selfies is my life! I want to be an Instagram influencer. My parents just don't understand; they think I'm just wasting my time. Especially my dad."

I heard what Melody was saying. And I appreciated her dream to be an Instagram influencer. But the real issue Melody needed to address first in treatment was the fact that she needed to get a job and needed to confront her feelings around this important life transition—moving into adulthood. Regardless of whatever career she decided to pursue. Spending all her time posting selfies all day long prevented her from doing just that and from working through all the complicated feelings and emotions that are bound to come up at Melody's stage of life.

Melody graduated from college a year before she'd begun working with me but still hadn't looked for a job. And moving back in with her parents, in the house she grew up in, was a hard adjustment. Melody described her mother as supportive; in fact, it was her mother who'd encouraged Melody to seek treatment. Melody's father, on the other hand, had not been as supportive of Melody's efforts to figure out her next step in adulthood, and this was a familiar role he played throughout her whole life.

Melody has a younger brother, whom she says is the star of the family and can do no wrong. This was especially true in her father's eyes.

"My brother's an amazing athlete. He's bright and takes all honors classes. And he's popular. The girls love him. My dad reminds me of how great my brother is all the time. He never says anything positive about me!"

Melody was confused, she was lacking in self-confidence, and she was desperately hungry for any and all forms of validation. She had close to a thousand followers on Instagram and always got a good amount of likes and positive comments on her posts. Yet even with all this online validation and admiration, Melody didn't feel good about herself, and she didn't know how to make herself feel better.

"I know people think I'm pretty, stylish, and cool from the responses I get from my Instagram account. And my followers admire me for what they perceive is courage to be out there by posting selfies. It's funny to me that my followers actually see me as someone who's full of self-confidence and happy with her life rather than the truth—that I'm angry most times and I'm afraid what my future will look like. I guess you could say Instagram is my pretend life. I can pretend to be something I'm not."

Although Melody was getting external validation from her Instagram account, it wasn't the kind she needed in order to move her life forward. What Melody needed to develop was internal validation. In short, she needed to work on building up her self-esteem. A big goal in treatment was to help Melody gain psychological insight in order for her to connect that she was using Instagram to boost her low self-esteem, to medicate her depression and the anger she held toward her emotionally neglectful father, and accept that her avoidance around getting a job was sabotaging her future. Helping Melody get to this point also meant she needed to develop and strengthen her emotional IQ. But first, let's explore what exactly emotional IQ is.

EMOTIONAL INTELLIGENCE IMPACTS SOCIAL MEDIA

Did you ever think back on something you posted online or even reflect on an important decisions you made in your life and wonder, "What was I thinking?" or "Did I really do that—and *why*?" Not using your emotional intelligence may be to blame for your rash behavior.

Emotional intelligence—or EQ—is the ability to identify and manage your own emotions as well as the emotions of others in an effective and positive way. People with high EQs are good communicators, modulate their emotions, are able to empathize with others, defuse conflicts, and are more adaptable to life's challenges.[5]

It's not hard to see how EQ can influence our social-media habits and even how successful we'll be in life. Of course our unique personal situations and intelligence are factors in our successes as well; however, EQ can profoundly affect our choices by creating options we may not have otherwise imagined or considered to be possibilities.

Emotional intelligence is comprised of the following skills.

- Self-awareness. This is the ability to label, recognize, and understand your own emotions. Self-awareness requires us to tune in to our feelings and not avoid our negative emotions, such as anxiety, fear, and sadness. Recognizing our own emotional states and how they affect our thoughts, behaviors, and decisions is key to cultivating self-awareness. As for digital self-awareness, you can increase this skill by getting into the habit of reviewing your social-media posts on a daily or weekly basis. When doing so, ask yourself questions like, "Do my posts accurately reflect my thoughts? My feelings? My values? My principals?" "Could I have unintentionally hurt someone's feelings?" Thinking about the effect your social-media contributions could have on other individuals and our society is crucial to developing self-awareness both online and off.

- Emotional regulation. This has to do with our ability to control strong emotions by not acting on raw feelings in an impulsive or destructive manner. Developing the ability to sit with unpleasant feelings to give us the time and space to decide how we may alleviate or reduce negative feelings cultivates self-confidence. Emotional regulation also helps us develop the ability to consider various solutions to a particular situation or problem. Not reacting solely from an emotionally charged state results in better decision-making outcomes. As for regulating our emotions in digital spaces, a good first step toward this goal is to simply pause before posting when emotional or about an emotional situation.

- Empathy. When we empathize with others, we develop deeper, more intimate relationships. Empathy is the ability to recognize how and why people feel the way they do. Empathy allows us to anticipate how our actions and behaviors influence other people, as well as ourselves. Developing empathy enhances our experiences and our relationships as well as a general understanding of ourselves, other people, and the world around us. Online you can apply this skill by regularly reviewing your news feeds, comments, and posts. Ask yourself, "Are my posts emotionally sensitive?" "Can they be interpreted as being disrespectful? Or Unkind?" "How would I feel if I were to get the same response?" "What could my friend possibly have been feeling when posting that sarcastic comment? Or posting a seductive picture of themselves?"

- Social skills. Very broadly, having strong social skills means having the ability to communicate in a clear, concise, and courteous manner. In a nutshell, good social skills are the summation of all of the components of EQ: self-awareness, emotional regulation, and empathy. Online social skills are just as important. Again, you can enhance your online social skills by regularly reviewing your profiles, newsfeeds, wall, posts, and comments. Check to make sure they reflect and project good digital citizenship—in other words, good digital social skills. As yourself, "Are my posts kind?" "Could my posts and comments be interpreted as being offensive or hurtful?" If so, go back to asking yourself, "How would I feel if someone were to comment and post something like that to *my* Facebook wall or any other social-networking site?"

BACK TO MELODY

In addition to developing Melody's emotional IQ, another goal I had for our work together was for her to develop the ability to mentalize. *Mentalization* is a psychological concept that refers to our capacity to perceive and interpret our and others' feelings, beliefs, needs, thoughts, and motivations that underlie overt behaviors.[6] Mentalization also has many of the same goals for cultivating and improving emotional IQ.

Mentalization is thought to be largely unconscious and intuitive, requiring us to imagine the mental thoughts of another person and the unconscious motives behind our own behavior. In short, mentalization requires us to self-reflect, something I believed would also greatly help Melody with understanding what was driving her compulsive need to post selfies on social media.

The first step in helping Melody become more skillful in the task of self-reflection was to start a "feelings journal" and get into the daily habit of writing down her feelings and the contexts in which they lived. Being able to accurately name and interpret our emotions is a crucial part of mentalization. This is because our emotions provide us with important information about our relationships, our behaviors, and the world around us. When we're in tune to our emotions, we can then use them to skillfully react to our environment and to the people in it. For example, when we're anxious about performing a specific task, like having to do a presentation, we will likely make sure we're as prepared as we can be. Or when we feel depressed, we might reach out to our friends more or engage in self-care activities that we know make us feel better. When we're not in tune with our emotions and our environment, we're more likely to act in ways that aren't as helpful for us.

As for Melody, as we began focusing on mentalization in our work together, she was quickly able to notice a pattern emerging around her selfie postings. Whenever she fought with her father or when her father made snide comments about her not yet finding a job and still living at home, Melody felt the urge to post a selfie on social media. After making this connection, it didn't take her long to realize that what she wanted most of all was her dad's admiration and emotional support—not the admiration of followers she didn't know and who knew nothing about her.

Learning how to skillfully resolve interpersonal conflict is another benefit of mentalizing. This is because mentalizing helps people to identify what it is they are feeling, learn how to verbalize their feelings, examine what brought about these feelings, notice what happened right before the feelings emerged, and, finally, carefully consider the consequences of their behaviors.

Melody and I agreed that having a few sessions with her father would be helpful. But before doing so, we worked on helping Melody develop more effective conflict-resolution skills—such as, assuming others don't know what we think, need, or want; being direct with our words; and clearly knowing the goals for our relationships.

Melody's father agreed to come, and Melody was able to articulate what she was feeling and what she needed from him emotionally. As Melody's relationship with her father grew and changed, her compulsive selfie posting dissipated. She then had time to look for a job, which she eventually found, and she was even able to move into an apartment of her own. Melody still posts selfies on Instagram and is still seriously considering being an Instagram influencer, but it's no longer her main source of validation.

HOW FEELING BAD CAN BE GOOD FOR US

As I mentioned earlier in this chapter, the act of self-medicating is driven by the desire to avoid our negative feelings. Negative feelings are disturbing and often times linked to the very memories, events, and circumstances we want to forget! We can all relate to the immediate relief avoidance can provide. However, this relief is temporary, and we pay a heavy price in the long term when we avoid acknowledging, examining, and accepting our negative emotions.

In actuality, our unpleasant and negative emotions—powerlessness, anger, depression, anxiety, and fear—are signals telling us something is wrong. When we avoid our emotions by using defense mechanisms—such as repression, minimization, fantasy, rationalization, projection, somatization, wishful thinking, and idealization—we miss the opportunity to make effective and helpful changes. Learning how to tolerate and experience our negative emotions rather than defending against them—for example, with compulsive social-media use, overeating, overdrinking, or compulsive pornography use—allows us to understand them and to then figure out what to do next that will help us. [7]

SKILL-BUILDING STRATEGIES

- Work on developing the ability to sit with your negative and unpleasant emotions like depression, anxiety, fear, and anger. We all experience these feelings at some time or another. Keep in mind that feelings pass. They have a beginning, middle, and end, so no matter how bad you feel now, you won't feel bad forever. Tolerating negative emotions, and accepting them as a natural part of life, is also important to being able to figure out healthy solutions.
- Be patient with yourself. It takes time to sort out complicated emotions and to understand the full circumstances surrounding them. Emotions are complicated, and we often feel several—sad, angry, anxious—all at the same time.

- Accept that negative emotions are normal and a part of being human. Our goal should not be to never feel bad. That's impossible. Instead, learning how to manage our negative emotions should be our focus and goal.
- It's okay to not react in response to your negative feelings. Impulsive reactions often make circumstances and feelings worse. Instead, try to slow down your reactions by being patient and allowing yourself the time to sort out what it is you're feeling and why. When you have a greater understanding of your feelings and the circumstances surrounding them, your reactions will be more effective and less damaging to you.

NOW WHAT?

Take a moment to ask yourself, "Am I using social media to medicate my negative feelings?" "Am I using social media to avoid confronting an upsetting circumstance in my current life? For example, do I feel stuck in an unhappy marriage? Or stuck in an unfulfilling career?" If you tested yourself using the Social Media Disorder Scale, did your scores reflect destructive social-media use? If you answered yes to any of the questions above, there's a good chance you're self-medicating an underlying issue with technology. In all of the years I've been in therapeutic practice, I've never witnessed problems disappearing on their own and without the hard work of self-examination. In short, continuing to use technology to numb feelings won't solve problems. We can't heal what we don't feel.

Cultivating self-awareness and the ability to name, regulate, and express our emotions—skills associated with emotional IQ and mentalizing—dramatically helps us address the challenges of life skillfully as opposed to destructively, like self-medicating with drugs, alcohol, shopping, pornography, or social media.

Following are some recommendations to help you get in touch with your feelings and better understand how paying attention to your emotional IQ and taking the time to work on developing it more, if need be, is important to your overall life, both online and off.

RECOMMENDATIONS

1. Cultivate self-awareness by regularly reviewing your social-media profiles, wall, pictures, posts, tweets, and news feeds. Ask yourself, "Do my posts reflect my principals? My values?" "Are they respectful?" "Could they be misconstrued to be hurtful or unkind?" Self-aware people are aware of how they can affect those around them. Practicing good citizenship is an example of digital self-awareness.[8]

2. Start a feelings journal. Journaling is a good way to discover patterns and helps reinforce our understanding that our feelings are a part of life. For example, perhaps you'll discover you're more likely to log on to social media when you're feeling left out or rejected by a friend or family member. Learning how to express your feelings to those you feel hurt by dramatically reduces the risk of self-medicating behaviors and increases your ability to resolve conflict. All of which leads to living a more skillful life!

3. Practice distress tolerance. Self-medicating behaviors result from an inability to calm ourselves down when we are feeling stressed. Learning how to manage stress and crisis in skillful ways that help without causing negative aftershocks is key. You can start to work on this skill by making a list of coping behaviors that you have used in the past that have helped. Remember, there's a difference between knowing and doing.[9]

7

A CALL FOR SELF-COMPASSION IN THE DIGITAL AGE

> Love and compassion are necessities, not luxuries. Without them humanity cannot survive.
>
> —attributed to the Dalai Lama[1]

Self-compassion plays a major role in our healing. In this chapter, you will learn about the three main components of self-compassion—self-kindness, common humanity, and mindfulness—and how these components can help protect you from the negative consequences of social media, such as FOMO, envy, and upward social comparisons.

You'll meet Sandi and John, two well-meaning people whose lack of self-compassion fuels their unhealthy patterns of social-media usage and takes them off course from living the lives they both desire and deserve. At the end of this chapter, you'll find prescriptive actions for cultivating self-compassion and self-love, such as celebrating personal achievements both big and small, comparing yourself only to yourself, and learning how to count personal blessings.

But first, what's self-compassion?

A PRIMER ON SELF-COMPASSION

Over and over again, studies show that practicing self-compassion enables us to lead lively and enriching lives. It increases levels of self-esteem and well-being and decreases malignant envy, depression, anxiety, hurtful social comparisons, and narcissism. Self-compassion is also an important ingredient for self-development, because it helps us recover from our mistakes, bounce back more quickly from life's inevitable setbacks, and achieve our goals.[2]

Compassion has its roots in Buddhism, an Eastern philosophy. In the classical teachings of the Buddhist tradition, *compassion* is defined as "the heart that trembles in the face of suffering." The aspiration to compassion is said to be the noblest quality of the human heart, the motivation underlying all meditative paths of healing, liberation, and forgiveness. Self-compassion is taking this concept one step further by applying it to ourselves.[3]

Why do we need to practice self-compassion? For many of us, our inner turmoil stems from negative talk—not believing we're good enough, berating ourselves when we make a mistake or fail to accomplish the things we expect we should, and scolding or shaming ourselves when we feel we do not fit into our ideal vision of ourselves. It's no surprise that our critical, negative internal dialogues are what create our emotional suffering in the form of depression, anxiety, substance abuse, emotional eating, isolation, toxic relationships, and even unhealthy social-media habits. The good news is that learning the skills of self-compassion is one way to overcome negative talk and improve your screen health.

MEET SANDI

Sandi, a sixty-year-old divorced and overweight woman, came to see me because she was desperate to lose weight, get healthy, and meet a "good man." Sandi had tried every fad diet out there with little to no success. Sandi's health was suffering as well; she had high blood pressure, was prediabetic, and had thyroid issues, which made losing weight more difficult for her.

Sandi had struggled with her weight ever since she was a young girl. Her mother thought nothing of slipping in an occasional negative comment about it, and her younger sister and peers teased her as well. Sandi's mother's comments often led to fights and arguments, making life feel chaotic and unstable.

Sandi had a secretive and hurtful habit that she relied on to cope with her negative emotions: binge eating while on social media. She referred to this behavior as her "guilty pleasure." In session, Sandi described spending hours of her day lying in bed, examining with great intensity the social-media profiles of her friends, her friends of friends, and even people she didn't know, all the while binge eating on sugary foods like donuts, peanut butter, ice cream, cookies, and sweet cereals.

Binge eating was not a new behavior for Sandi. She had been using food to medicate her feelings since she was a teenager. But being on social media while in the throes of a binge-eating episode was a new behavior, and it magnified her feelings of shame tenfold. Sandi's critical inner voice was telling her how bad she was for binge eating while at the same time telling her that she was a complete failure compared to her virtual "friends" and "followers," heaping extra servings of shame onto her psyche.

If Sandi came in to see me for our appointment the day after a night of this, she'd always start the session telling me,

"I hate myself!"
"I'm disgusting!"
"I'll never find a man!"
"I'll be alone for the rest of my life!"
"No one wants a fat woman!"
"Everyone on social media is happy!"
"My mom is right—I'll never be in a relationship looking this way!"
"How can you even stand to look at me??"

Sandi didn't know how to pull back from her destructive eating episodes without mentally beating herself up and making herself feel even worse. Shaming ourselves or another person for an undesirable behavior doesn't lead to motivation, initiation, or change. In fact, this vicious cycle of binge-shame-binge even prevented Sandi from advancing in her profession and from forming positive and mutually satisfying romantic relationships, because it depleted her emotionally and intellectually. And Sandi's unacknowledged and unaddressed feelings of shame also made it more likely that she'd repeat this behavior again and again; in a nutshell, we can't heal what we don't know we feel.

Kristin Neff, psychologist and leading expert in the study of compassion and self-compassion, breaks self-compassion down into the following three components: self-kindness, common humanity, and mindfulness. Let's now examine each one.

SELF-KINDNESS IN PLACE OF SELF-JUDGMENT

Neff defines *self-kindness* as the ongoing, never-ending quest to understand in a kind, open, and curious way rather than having an attitude of harsh judgment, self-criticism, and defensiveness. Our personal flaws and inadequacies are treated in a gentle, understanding manner when we adopt an attitude of self-kindness, and the emotional tone of the language we use toward ourselves is loving, tender, kind, and supportive, making us more accepting of our imperfections. Similarly, when external life circumstances are difficult, self-compassionate people turn inward to offer themselves soothing and comfort rather than taking a stoic "Just grin and bear it" approach. An example of practicing self-compassion that Dr. Neff recommends is giving yourself a big hug when facing a difficult situation or actually telling yourself, "I'm so sorry, honey."[4]

The emotional benefit derived from self-compassion is not a new concept to the world of psychology and psychotherapy. Much of the aim of successful traditional psychotherapy treatment for disorders such as depression, anxiety, obsessive-compulsive personality disorder, eating disorders, body-image disorders, borderline personality disorder, and substance abuse is to "soften" rigid, inflexible, and punitive superegos. Our *superego*, based on Freud's theories, is the part of our mind that acts as our self-critical conscience, reflecting the social standards we learned from our parents, teachers, and other important adult role models. A harsh superego, manifested in our harsh critical internal voice, causes us to feel feelings like shame and inferiority.[5] These kinds of feelings, more times than not, leave us emotionally frozen or depleted. Conversely, a balanced and gentle superego takes the form of a kinder and more realistic inner voice. In a nutshell, an inner voice that's compassionate means less emotional turmoil and realistic self-appraisals and leads to emotional openness and feelings of hopefulness.

Cognitive behavioral therapy, another well-known treatment approach to various mental and emotional disorders, seeks to help clients put their inner critical voices in perspective by challenging critical internal dialogues with self-compassionate self-talk. Techniques such as *re-framing* (rethinking our negative thoughts by challenging them) soften the inner critic by replacing negative thoughts with ones that offer a healthy perspective and balance.[6]

Founded by British clinical psychologist Paul Gilbert and based off of Neff's groundbreaking work in self-compassion, *compassion-focused therapy* is an integrative therapeutic approach developed for people who specifically struggle with chronic and complex mental-health problems stemming from self-shame and self-criticism, often people who come from neglectful or abusive backgrounds. CFT, as it is known, borrows its from Buddhist teachings—especially the roles of sensitivity to and motivation to relieve suffering—but its roots derive from an evolutionary, neuroscience, and social-psychology approach, emphasizing the psychology and neurophysiology of both giving and receiving care.[7]

An interesting pattern in the health domain has emerged that shows a link between self-compassion and a reduction in disordered eating, shame, perfectionism, and body dissatisfaction. For example, an innovative study investigated the impact that viewing fitspiration images (images that serve as motivation for someone to sustain or improve health and fitness) and viewing self-compassion quotations had on the body image and mood of women social-media users. The results suggest that actively viewing social-media accounts supporting self-compassion might offer a novel approach to attenuating the negative impact of social media on women's body satisfaction. Representations of self-compassion are abundant on social media. As of June 2020, the hashtag #selfcompassion yielded over 599,000 Instagram images. These self-compassion images feature quotes such as, "It's okay to do what's best for you," "I think you are doing a beautiful job figuring out some heavy sh#t," "Strive for progress," and "Do things with kindness."[8]

BACK TO SANDI

Sandi and I did work together around identifying her feelings of shame, where they originated, and how to reframe them in a self-compassionate context by replacing her critical self-talk with loving, tender, and kind phrases and words of advice. To do this yourself, think along the lines of what you would say to a good friend in a similar situation; Sandi would never berate a friend for a binge-eating episode the way she berated herself. In digital spaces, Sandi explored social media from the perspective of self-compassion by searching sites like Instagram and Facebook for inspirational and self-affirming accounts that resonated with her journey toward leading a healthy lifestyle and cultivating self-compassion. The accounts she followed posted inspirational quotes on a daily basis. She would make sure to start her day by reading from those she found most helpful. She would either write down quotes she found on social media that were particularly inspiring or print them out and place them in her journal.

Over time Sandi was able to create a kinder, gentler, self-dialogue through talk therapy and social media. Being more self-compassionate helped her to lose weight and reduced the frequency of her binge-eating episodes. Sandi also gained the confidence to discuss the possibility of getting promoted at work, and she began dating a man she finally felt good about.

LET GO OF SHAME FOR A HAPPIER YOU

Let's be honest: we've all done things that we're ashamed of. Shame is a universal human emotion. Most psychologists say that a healthy dose of shame, when rightfully felt, is beneficial to our well-being and relationships. It keeps us on track for behaving in "socially appropriate" ways so we maintain our relationships and repair them when necessary.

However, chronic and unnecessary feelings of self-directed shame are exhausting, paralyzing, and toxic to our emotional health. Shame of this kind is typically rooted in deep-seated feelings of inferiority, inadequacy, and defectiveness, and the degree to which these shameful feelings are felt most times doesn't match the reality of the situation that caused them in the first place.

It's important to know the difference between feelings of unhealthy shame and feelings of guilt. *Guilt* reflects emotions related to doing something wrong or bad, whereas *shame* reflects feeling fundamentally bad about yourself regardless of the situation or circumstance. Those struggling with deep-seated, unhealthy feelings of shame tend to withdraw and hide from the world, only to be left feeling even lonelier and rejected.

SKILL-BUILDING STRATEGIES

Overcoming shame and rebuilding self-esteem and self-love takes time and patience, but it can be done. Below are a few strategies to help get you started.

- Commit to making self-compassion a daily practice. We are more likely to be critical of ourselves when we feel shame, but harsh self-talk only intensifies our shameful feelings. One way to practice self-compassion is by treating yourself as you would a good friend. Neff suggests using self-talk that includes words like *honey* and *dear* and using physical touch such as giving yourself hugs.
- Identify situations and people both online and off that trigger feelings of shame. There may be people in our lives that we notice reinforce or trigger our feelings of shame. When this happens, it could be a warning sign of a dysfunctional relationship. Give yourself permission to reduce or eliminate the time spent with those who make you feel ashamed. Remember, the hallmarks of healthy relationships are love, respect, and compassion.
- Don't heap on unnecessary layers of shame. We all experience feelings of shame; give yourself permission to feel shame when you feel it. But avoid heaping more hurt and shame onto yourself by being harsh and self-critical about your feelings in the first place. When we accept our feelings, we stop fighting against them, giving ourselves the emotional space to begin the work of understanding and addressing the underlying causes of our shame.

COMMON HUMANITY VERSUS ISOLATION

The second healing component of self-compassion is common humanity. When practicing self-compassion, feelings of common humanity and belongingness automatically occur within us. We reduce feelings of separation and isolation and, in turn, depression and a host of other emotional disorders when we learn to see our interpersonal and intrapersonal experiences as part of the larger human experience rather than seeing "bad things and bad experiences" as only happening to us.[9] The truth is, we all make mistakes and go through difficult times. Even experiencing life's celebrations and good times with feelings of separateness and disconnection from humanity can also bring about feelings of isolation and disconnection. Hence the phrase, "It's lonely at the top."

As we've seen, studies of social media seemingly conflict: some suggest that social media—from Facebook to Twitter to Instagram to Snapchat—has made us more connected, while others suggest we are more lonely and more narcissistic than ever before. It's more likely that the truth is somewhere in the middle. That is, social media at times has made people feel both more connected and more lonely. As for feelings of loneliness, lonely people are in fact more prone to depression, anxiety, and substance abuse. A few studies investigating social media suggest that Facebook users had slightly lower levels of "social loneliness"—the sense of not feeling bonded with friends—but "significantly higher levels of family loneliness"—the sense of not feeling bonded with family. These researchers also find that lonely people are inclined to spend more time on Facebook per day as opposed to nonlonely individuals.[10] Furthermore, since social media provokes feelings of envy, FOMO, and upward and downward social comparisons, it can also lead to defensive reactions and interactions. Defensive reactions aren't likely to produce warm and fuzzy emotional interactions, making us feel connected. Rather, they are quite the opposite: most defensive reactions wall us off psychologically, leaving us to feel more alone, separate, and cutoff.

BREAKING DOWN WALLS, LETTING GO, AND MOVING ON AS A BY-PRODUCT OF SELF-COMPASSION

Letting go is hard. Whether you've missed a deadline at work, made a hurtful comment to a friend or family member online or offline, or been unfaithful in your relationship, constantly berating yourself and spending sleepless nights reliving the experience doesn't help you learn from your mistakes, forgive yourself, or move on.

Social media can also provoke feelings that are hard to let go of, because they trigger deeper emotions. In our 24-7 world of constant tweets, Instagram posts, Facebook likes, and YouTube stars telling us how to look, feel, act, and be, it's harder and harder to not compare ourselves to others in digital spaces and to fight off unwarranted feelings of inadequacy, inferiority, or lacking.

But it's not all bad news! The mere act of acknowledging our feelings like envy, anger, frustration, and sadness with an attitude of self-compassion is key for being able to let go of negative emotions.

SKILL-BUILDING STRATEGIES

There's no doubt that letting go, forgiving others, forgiving ourselves, and moving on is hard. It means accepting the reality that we and those we love have imperfections and faults.

Below are tips to help you cultivate the art of letting go of life's big and small disappointments and stressors.

- Acknowledge your feelings. No matter how minor a disappointment or stressor may seem to you, it's important to acknowledge your feelings. Calling a friend or relative to let off some steam can quickly reduce the intensity of anger, frustration, and sadness. Small stressors that go unacknowledged and unexpressed pile up and, at some point, begin to take their toll.
- Mindfully accept your emotions. If a picture, post, or tweet stirs up feelings of inadequacy or envy, accept your feelings instead of suppressing or avoiding them. Respond to your

feelings with words and thoughts of kindness, all the while holding in mind the reality that imperfection is a part of the human experience for everyone—even those on social media we envy.

- Pull away from screens. At times, the most self-compassionate response to feeling overwhelmed by negative emotions is to step back and take a break from whatever has left you feeling so badly. For example, seeing photos of an ex on social media after a fresh breakup would be overwhelming for anyone. Stepping away from your screen and engaging in self-care practices like drinking tea, deep-breathing exercises, taking a warm bath, or petting a beloved dog or cat can be a powerful form of self-care.

- Put the disappointment into perspective. Putting some degree of emotional distance between yourself and the circumstance can help. Neff recommends asking yourself, "What would I say to a friend facing this problem?" "Would the event seem minor or moderate?" Putting things into perspective helps with gaining an understanding about whether or not your emotional reaction is helpful or even necessary.

- Be patient with yourself. Acknowledging our feelings is work and can be emotionally draining, especially if this personal work is something new and unfamiliar to you. Developing self-compassion takes time and patience. It's an adaptive and necessary skill to have in order to lead a happier and healthier life.

- Stick with it; it will be worth it. Find ways to quickly reduce your stress and anxiety. Find a stress-reduction method that works for you. Mindfulness meditation, yoga, and deep breathing have all been shown to be effective stress-reducing techniques.

MINDFULNESS VERSUS OVERIDENTIFICATION

The third and final component of self-compassion is mindfulness. In the context of self-compassion, mindfulness refers to holding onto our painful thoughts and emotions with balanced awareness. Sweeping our bad feelings and thoughts under the rug rarely if ever makes them go away. In fact, more often than not, these futile attempts do the exact opposite: they make our negative emotions and thoughts louder, more intrusive, and more painful. On the other hand, neither does it help to pretend we don't feel our negative feelings, by minimizing them and telling ourselves, "I'm really fine" or "It doesn't affect me in the least" when in reality we're crushed and heartbroken. Pretending we don't feel makes our emotions harder to bear. In short, undigested, unprocessed, and unacknowledged emotions make us sicker, not better. And to repeat what I stated earlier, we can't heal what we don't feel.

Balanced awareness is felt when we avoid overly identifying or wallowing in our negative emotional states; our feelings are neither repressed nor exaggerated. In order to find balanced awareness, we need to create what can be thought of as a "healing distance" between our feelings and the actual situation that spurred our upset.

From a psychoanalytic perspective, balanced awareness is akin to what is known as a balanced *observing ego*. The observing ego is the part of our consciousness that mediates our capacity for self-reflection, learning, and morality.[11] A healthy observing ego allows us to be present, prosocial, thoughtful, and intentional in our actions and behaviors. Excessive self-observation, on the other hand, can lead to crippling self-consciousness and shame, whereas diminished observing-ego or balanced-awareness function can result in antisocial behaviors, identity disturbances, and feelings of depersonalization (a disconnection from ourselves).

MEET JOHN

At forty-two years old, John had a lot to be angry about. He was on the verge of losing his high-power and high-earning job as an investment banker, his marriage was on shaky ground, and he was caring for his sickly father with whom he'd had a difficult relationship his entire life.

As a way to displace his anger, John would insult and berate his wife, the main reason John's marriage was in jeopardy. Another way John displaced his anger was by logging on to Twitter, Facebook, Instagram, and random message boards, under a fake name, and intentionally provoking people from his anonymous profile by posting sarcastic, insulting, and hurtful comments and threads. None of his family or friends knew he was doing this. It was something John did in complete secrecy.

"I know this is messed up," John told me one day in session, "and I want to figure out better ways to deal with my anger!"

> As a kid, my dad teased and tormented me. If I told him I had a setback in school, like when I did poorly on an exam or got into a fight with another kid in my class, he'd always respond with an insult. I remember he'd say things like, "Don't be a sissy!" "I bet you got the crap beaten out of you!" "Stop whining like a girl!"
>
> There were plenty of times my father's verbal assaults seemed to have come out of nowhere! As a kid, I assumed it was my fault—that somehow I was to blame and therefore I deserved to be punished and yelled at. But, I'm now learning that's not true. My father was the parent, the adult, and it was his responsibility to find mature ways to deal with his anger. I'd bet my entire savings his father did the same to him.

REPETITIONS, ENACTMENTS, AND SOCIAL MEDIA

There was no question about it—John's childhood had been traumatic. People who have been victimized or traumatized often try to cope and cover up their wounded feelings by being aggressive and domineering in their relationships with others. And John was right to assume his father had suffered a similar miserable childhood with his own father. It's this same cycle of family abuse that explains why school bullies have often been victims of bullying themselves.

The defense mechanism—identifying with the aggressor, briefly stated—describes the process by which a victim of abuse internalizes and adopts the behaviors of their abuser. An extreme example of this is Stockholm syndrome: in these cases, the victim seeks to avoid abuse by creating an emotional connection with their abuser in hopes that the abuser will develop feelings of empathy and relatedness toward the abused, thereby decreasing the chances of abuse and increasing chances of survival. [12]

BACK TO JOHN

We are all destined to repeat toxic dynamics from childhood that we haven't yet uncovered, understood, and healed. This type of repetition in our behavior is what psychologists refer to as an *enactment*. John was fundamentally replicating what his father had originally done to him when he lashed out and was abusive over social media. He'd post demeaning comments to people, telling them they were "stupid," "idiots," "losers," or "weak-minded," repeating the cruel words his father had said to him when he'd been a young boy and teen.

The first step in John's healing was to help him acknowledge, in a self-compassionate context, the pain his father's verbal abuse had caused him. The second step involved helping John to see how his insulting comments would make a person on the receiving end feel. Calling another person, "stupid" or an "idiot" is hurtful, whether it's said online or off. When we fully appreciate the extent to which we have hurt another, we move toward healthy feelings of regret and the healthy desire to want to make reparations, the making of amends for a wrong we've done another. This process of empathetic, imaginative reflection was also extended to John's mistreatment of his wife too.

Helping John cultivate balanced awareness and develop his observing ego not only made him more aware of how his comments could make other people feel online, it also improved his relationships offline—especially his relationship with his wife. John learned to develop the capacity for self-compassion and compassion for all. This even extended to his father. This new awareness was also positive for his career. He got along better with his coworkers and his supervisor, all of which improved his employment security.

MENDING WALLS

I believe it's safe to say that all psychologists will agree that teaching clients self-compassion leads to tremendous healing and growth. Most times we aren't able to take care of ourselves from a place of self-compassion because we weren't treated in a compassionate way as young children, so we repeat the dynamic with others and ourselves. The research on self-compassion also shows it to be a crucial component to forgiveness for both ourselves and others. This practice reaps dividends not only in our offline lives but in our online lives as well.

Exercising self-compassion and compassion for all people online is just as important and can contribute to healing on a global level. With the rise in hate speech and cyberbullying and the climbing numbers of teen suicides, it is imperative that as a society, nation, and world we recognize the urgent call for cultivating online digital compassion.

Most will agree that tragic events taking place via social media don't stem from users being too compassionate, too mindful of their emotions, too understanding of how their actions and behaviors affect others, too empathetic, or too concerned over the success of the human race. We can all play our part in the solution by first helping ourselves and then teaching others. Imagine a digital world where we elevate the dialogue to the degree that compassion is engendered, where disagreements played out online enlighten us all instead of breaking us down, where the best of humanity is showcased in place of the very worst.

As great author Leo Tolstoy said, everyone thinks of changing the world, but no one thinks of changing himself. [13]

Below are some ideas to help you start on the path toward implementing self-compassion, both online and off.

RECOMMENDATIONS

1. Make sense of your past. It's never okay to make negative comments to or about others. If you find yourself engaged in digital confrontations, examine your family history. It's common for people to reenact dysfunctional relational dynamics. Left unexamined, sadly, these behaviors rarely change.
2. Learn to identify the ways in which social media can support your journey of self-compassion. Spend some time exploring social media from the perspective of self-compassion. Choose to follow accounts that are inspirational and affirming.
3. If you find yourself being pulled down by negative thoughts and feelings while scrolling through social media, recognize that this could be an opportunity for you to practice self-compassion versus indulging in hurtful social comparisons.

4. Celebrate personal achievements, both big and small, and count your blessings. Cultivating gratitude and appreciating our achievements helps us avoid the trap of overidentifying with negative emotions or exaggerating difficult circumstances.

8

FINDING YOUR E-TRIBE

Call it a clan, call it a network, call it a tribe, call it a family. Whatever you call it, whoever you are, you need one.

—Jane Howard[1]

Whether it's a family, a substitute family, a community, a religious organization, a gardening club, a book club, or a professional association, it's well established that being a part of a group or tribe is crucial for our emotional development and well-being. In fact, statistics and research support the fact that our social connections and participation in groups enrich and add meaning to our lives and decrease our risks for depressive disorders, anxiety, substance abuse, loneliness, and low self-esteem. Furthermore, there's also reason to believe that "social connectedness" is at least as good for your health as exercising or quitting smoking. It aids recovery from physical and mental illness and provides resilience in the face of stressful life events and transitions.[2]

As I was writing this book, Facebook launched its new ad campaign More Together, which featured groups of people connecting with slogans like, "We're More Unstoppable Together," "We're More Intergalactic Together," and "Whatever You're Into, There's A Group for You." These ads encourage Facebook users to expand their digital social network from individual virtual friendships to include various Facebook groups based on interests, from gardening to superhero comic books. In many ways, Facebook's campaign gets it right. As Helen Keller famously said, "Alone we can do so little; together we can do so much."[3]

In an era when we have enough tools and devices at our fingertips to connect us 24-7, one would think loneliness would be on the decline. Yet studies show we're lonelier than ever. At the same time, there's research indicating that, when used in specific ways, social media can have a positive impact on well-being and belongingness. In this chapter, you'll meet Jackie, a middle-aged widow who, despite digital advances for connecting, hasn't been able to form meaningful friendships. You'll also meet Riley, a millennial who grew up in a dysfunctional family and who is on the search, both online and off, for people who can stand in like "family." This chapter ends with suggestions for how social media can be used to reflect our authentic selves, incorporate positive shared experiences, and promote belonging.

THE DRIVE TO BELONG

People who struggle with feelings of belongingness often say,

> "I feel like an outsider."
> "People don't care about me."
> "I feel disconnected from the rest of the world."
> "I feel alone even when I'm with other people."
> "My family and friends rarely include me in their plans."
> "My social-media profile looks like I have lots of friends. But in reality, I never actually talk to anyone IRL."

People across all cultures, religions, racial groups, economic groups, and genders have an innate drive to form relationships that are enduring, positive, and meaningful. The belongingness hypothesis, formulated by psychologists Roy Baumeister and Mark Leary, suggests that our most satisfying relationships are made up of frequent, affectionate, and reciprocal interactions with the same people over a span of time, as opposed to interactions with numerous and interchangeable people. Baumeister and Leary also say that we exert a great deal of time and emotional energy gratifying our fundamental drives to form relationships.[4] It's no wonder that social media is ubiquitous: it perfectly couples technology with our instinct to connect and belong.

Abraham Maslow's theory of what motivates humans, as expressed in his hierarchy of needs, discussed in chapter 1, also echoes many of the sentiments of the belongingness hypothesis. Our need for acceptance, love, and belonging fall right after our basic needs for safety, food, water, rest, and shelter.[5] Both Maslow's hierarchy and the belongingness hypothesis indicate that our need for belonging and love is based on our shared humanity and exist beyond our geographic, racial, gender, social, ethnic, and religious boundaries.

When we talk about relational issues like belonging, it's impossible to leave out Bowlby's theories on attachment. His work highlights that, although humans are built to form relationships, our attachments need to be secure and emotionally healthy in order for us to thrive throughout our lives.[6] This is because secure attachments free up our minds to learn and concentrate, inoculates us against toxic stress, teaches us how to regulate our emotions, provide examples of prosocial behaviors, set the foundation for a healthy sense of self, and lead to self-reliance and self-esteem. Anxious and avoidant attachments, on the other hand, hold us back to the degree that they do because anxious and avoidant attached individuals are preoccupied with their conflicted and hostile relationships, taking up precious space in their heads, interfering with their ability to learn and grow. It's not a surprise to learn that, for these individuals, despite living in an age where "connecting" is ubiquitous, forming harmonious and meaningful relationships is a lifelong struggle.

MEET JACKIE

Jackie, a forty-five-year-old widow and mother of a college-age daughter, lives alone and has no friends to speak of. She works as an administrator for her local school district.

"I never had friends growing up," she told me one day in session. "And I can say with certainty that I've never had a best friend. I like to believe this is because I was a shy child. But the truth is, that's only one part of the problem: I push people away because I'm so afraid of rejection."

Growing up, Jackie never felt like she belonged anywhere. Instead, she mostly felt rejected, and she greatly feared that showing people her "true self" would be humiliating for her. In fact, Jackie had ample reason to feel this way. Her father often teased her, telling her she was adopted. He even went so far as to show Jackie fake adoption papers to make her believe his cruel joke.

After experiencing such hurtfulness from a parent, it's no wonder Jackie struggled with forming relationships both as a child and later as an adult. She carried within herself intense rage and powerful images from her past that caused her to treat everyone she met as if they were her father. In psychotherapy, this kind of reaction—redirecting feelings formed in childhood to a new person—is called *transference*. Jackie believed people would reject her just as her father had, so she behaved in ways that she thought would protect her. Emotionally, she was very guarded and tended to shut people out. Her guardedness and cautiousness were also reflected in her avoidant attachment style. Jackie felt she had to hide her "true self" because she feared that I and others would end up rejecting her—or worse, humiliating her—by teasing her for having normal emotions such as uncertainty, fear, shame, sadness or for having the normal need to be admired, loved, and feel special.

As a consequence of her early relationship with her father, Jackie often teased coworkers and family members to the point where her teasing crossed the line from merely playful to cruel. Because it was hard for Jackie to recognize this behavior in herself, she struggled to form and maintain relationships. She blamed others for being too thin-skinned when they got upset or angry with her disrespectful behaviors and comments.

For Jackie, as for many people, social media's capacity to be a preliminary step toward experiencing belonging through new and healthy relationships can be transformative. Like any social gatherings, social media is a place that naturally facilitates connections between users based on shared interests, activities, or characteristics. Users can share and exchange information individually through online communities and networks like LinkedIn, Facebook, and Twitter.

Jackie's deficits in social skills made her feel awkward, out of place, and self-conscious when she was around other people. These feelings also prevented Jackie from making meaningful connections. I believed social media could offer her, from a comfortable distance, the opportunity to observe, learn, and model prosocial skills and healthy interactions that she hadn't learned for her parents during her childhood. Observing and thereby taking in positive digital interactions—what psychologists refer to as *internalizations*—gave Jackie ideas and options that she could apply to social situations both online and off.

But it's essential to use social media for therapeutic use in healthy ways. While it may be a beneficial tool, social media also has its limitations. The majority of information shared online is public, so it's important that you carefully consider how much personal information you want to share online and that you be thoughtful and realistic about the risks involved with oversharing on social media. Privacy is a genuine concern when using social media. It's important to make sure appropriate privacy settings are in place. Finally, while we are in control of what we post online, we cannot control how others may respond to it. Have a plan in place to cope with the possibility of negative reactions from others online.

Let's now examine the steps Jackie put in place to boost her sense of belonging.

FIND YOUR E-TRIBE

The most obvious answer for getting started on the path to finding your e-tribe is to create an online profile or identity. But for those struggling with social anxiety, depression, low self-esteem, or fear of rejection, putting yourself out there in the virtual world is just as difficult as it is in real life. This was certainly the case for Jackie.

As her therapist, what I believed would help her most was the experience of a tribe—that is, having people in her life who would fully embrace and accept her. New experiences and relationships of this type would contradict what Jackie had experienced from her rejecting father and family of origin. Through social media, Jackie could experience new opportunities for relationships that offer her emotional understanding, empathy, and caring.

Relationships and experiences that offer us healthy contradictory experiences, including therapeutic ones, are what psychologists refer to as *corrective emotional experiences*. In fact, corrective emotional experiences are thought to be the primary mechanisms for producing transformative and positive changes. Corrective emotional experiences are what happen when you experience something firsthand that challenges a previously held false or distorted belief.[7] For example, Jackie held a deep-seated belief that people would humiliate and reject her, a belief she formed based on her childhood experiences and relationship with her father. A corrective relationship for Jackie would be with others who are reliable in their ability to offer emotional support, encouragement, and understanding in place of teasing and humiliation.

One of my goals for Jackie was to have social media be a place where she would be able to find acceptance, encouragement, and support. For example, I imagined Jackie receiving supportive responses and comments on a post about having a rough day at work—something like, "Hope you have a relaxing night after such a tough day" or "Bad days are rough for me too. I have my go-to sweets for my TLC." For Jackie, these comments could be transformative because they would show her that she's not alone with her feelings and that other people *do* care about her—and that they're able to express their concern for her well-being in supportive and kind ways.

With my guidance, Jackie took that first step, establishing her online presence by creating a social-media profile. For Jackie to benefit from future social-media exchanges in the way I hoped, she needed for her profile to be authentic and truly representative of who she is. I encouraged her to engage in self-reflection in order to identify what aspects of herself—for example, her hobbies, tastes, education, and personal background—she would feel comfortable sharing on various social-media platforms like Instagram, LinkedIn, and Facebook. Specifically, Jackie and I discussed naming in her profile the university she'd attended, because, as she told me, "Out of all the schools I attended, I felt the most accepted while at college." Including Jackie's college in her profile would give her the chance to reconnect with old classmates and boost her feelings of belonging by deepening her connection to her alma mater and community. In addition, Jackie loved reading, music, and cooking. With this in mind, she began to explore the idea of following profiles, sites, or Facebook groups like The Cook's Cook Community Forum, NYT Cooking Community Public Group, Goodreads, and Instagram accounts that shared her interests in cooking and reading and consider how sharing her personal information with these accounts and commenting and liking posts boosted her feelings of connectedness and belonging.

Finally, creating her profile and listing her accomplishments was in itself therapeutic. Through this exercise, Jackie was able to "get to know herself," and in doing so her self-esteem and self-worth improved. She no longer had that constant feeling of being on the outside or fear of being rejected. Over time, as Jackie interacted with other people online who shared her interest in cooking and reading, she felt less and less alone with her feelings, which made her feel more connected to humanity as a whole.

"The friends I've made online share about their difficulties too," she told me. "They don't just post about the amazing things they're doing or how great their family is. This is a big deal for me, because even though to an outsider it was so obvious my dad had issues, he never acknowledged them. So I never felt able to discuss my problems either. The message was, you didn't talk about your problems or issues. I now know that attitude is not just wrong; it's also unhealthy and unhelpful."

This new insight and awareness helped Jackie express and therefore deal with complicated feelings head-on—like shame, sadness, and disappointment—rather than projecting these feelings onto others or denying and repressing them. Jackie gradually came to understand that her father had suffered psychological traumas that led him to behave in hurtful and destructive ways. Jackie slowly developed authentic relationships where she could be herself both online and offline.

Research studies show that people with depression, social anxiety, or any other mental illnesses report emotional benefits derived from online peer interactions. By sharing personal stories and strategies for coping with the day-to-day challenges of living with a mental illness, they experience greater social connectedness, feelings of group belonging, and hope. By learning from peers online, individuals with a mental illness may gain insight into important health-care decisions and treatments, all of which could promote positive mental-health-care-seeking behaviors. These individuals could also access interventions for psychological and physical well-being delivered through social media that could incorporate mutual support between peers, help promote treatment engagement, challenge the stigma associated with mental illness, and reach a broader demographic.[8]

Another study, examining the effects of online support for those going through treatment for breast cancer, showed that breast cancer patients' perceived knowledge increased and anxiety decreased by participation in a Twitter support group.[9]

Our sense of belonging and deep connection with others isn't just based on sharing our vulnerabilities or our real thoughts and feelings. Sharing lived experiences—like enjoying a holiday party or dinner, visiting a museum, attending a concert or a movie, or running a race with a close friend or family member—are also vital to forming deep bonds. This holds for our online interactions as well: sharing our good news on social-media platforms also can deepen ties and attachments with friends and family.

A second factor linked to deepening attachments in the context of shared experiences, online or off, is the reaction we receive from the person with whom we share and to whom we tell our experiences. When responses from others are positive, supportive, and enthusiastic, and when they match our emotions, we feel more connected.[10]

The psychological benefit derived from shared experiences is not a new understanding. Aristotle, ancient Greek philosopher and father of Western philosophy, wrote extensively on the topic of friendship. In his examination of friendship and what makes one a good friend, Aristotle highlights the concept of shared experiences and shared ideas and values as a means of deepening relationships. In short, friends are friends because there are things that they enjoy doing together; in Aristotle's words, they are joined in some "shared activity." Whatever we believe the goal of life to be, says Aristotle, that is the goal we will want to pursue with our friends.[11]

The positive influence of shared experiences on our emotional well-being and connectedness has also been supported by a few recent studies. For example, one such study found that shared experiences—even with a complete stranger—are experienced more intensely than are solo experiences. Another study underscored the positive effects of sharing experiences with those with whom we're already close, as opposed to those with whom we're not as close. In other words, the closer we feel to the person with whom we share an experience, the more enjoyable that experience will be for us.[12]

SKILL-BUILDING STRATEGY

Sharing positive experiences online with our virtual friends and family can also have positive effects on our sense of belonging, self-esteem, and emotional well-being. Below are three tips to help you get the most from your digital interactions.

- Share smaller accomplishments and experiences. These are just as important as sharing more significant life events. Posting about something on a smaller scale can be just as wonderful—like, "Had a great day catching up with an old friend" or "Got to see a beautiful sunset today" or "Had a great run this morning after weeks on my back!" Positive comments, likes, and shares on social media prolong our positive feelings associated with whatever "happy" moment we shared. When we read another's comment, even days later, we automatically reflect on our happy memory! These comments can be corrective emotional experiences.
- Include and tag close friends and family when sharing positive experiences online. Take pictures during a shared experience, and save them for posting later. This engenders digital interaction. Consider using hashtags to generate even more digital communications.
- Comment on other people's posts. Healthy relationships are reciprocal both online and off. Being social online is not easy for everyone, but it's crucial for benefiting from shared experiences and for cultivating a sense of belonging online.

BROKEN FAMILIES AND BELONGING

For all people, their first experience of belonging to something greater than themselves is with their family. If they are fortunate enough to have been raised by "good-enough parents or caregivers" and therefore formed secure attachments, they will have a well-established sense of belonging in their psyche.

Good-enough parents is a term derived from the work of well-known British pediatrician and psychoanalysis D. W. Winnicott, who was particularly influential in the fields of developmental psychology and object-relations theory. Winnicott's theory rests on the concept that an "average expectable environment" is essential for us to develop the necessary skills for relatedness.[13] *Relatedness* refers to the social nature of human beings that drives us to form connections with others. The sense of belonging that is planted and grows within a child from a loving and reliable relationship with their parents lasts for a lifetime and sets the foundation upon which all the child's later growth and relationships will build. The parental relationship is the foundation from which we can extend outward into the larger world.[14]

The majority of shared experiences in securely attached and healthy families with parents, caregivers, and extended family are likely to have been positive and supportive, with caregivers and parents who were emotionally attuned, empathetic, and available. Being raised in this type of environment results in a healthy sense of agency, self-esteem, and belonging.

Conversely, and not surprisingly, those raised in dysfunctional families have had more negative shared experiences with their families than positive ones, thus often resulting in lifelong struggles with feelings of belonging. Psychologists recognize the importance and influence of early childhood trauma on adult behavior. If not healed, early emotional childhood wounds will play out destructively on our direction through and reaction to life.

Codependency—a common symptom of dysfunctional families, originally referring to patterns of interactions associated in families with alcoholism or other substance-abuse disorders—describes a set of behaviors and attitudes in which the codependent is wholly preoccupied with and feels responsible for another person's well-being. The term has gradually broadened to include family dynamics that rely heavily on denial, shame-based rules, the avoidance of confrontation, and the inability to develop healthy resolutions to conflict. Recently psychologists and other mental-health professionals have learned that codependent behaviors can also contribute to the formation of dysfunctional families in general and isn't just a risk among families already struggling with addiction or substance abuse. Therefore, addressing codependent behavior in treatment is crucial for establishing a healthy family dynamic. [15]

Some common behaviors and signs associated with codependency follow.

- The need for excessive approval from other people
- Organizing thoughts and actions around others' perceived expectations and desires
- An overly defined sense of responsibility for others' happiness and emotional well-being
- The inability to express one's real thoughts and feelings for fear it will upset others
- The dependence of one's identity and self-esteem on others' approval and assumed expectations

Fortunately, codependency is a learned behavior and can be changed with therapy.

Let's now turn our attention to learn about how Riley, a young man struggling with belongingness and codependent characteristics, used social media to overcome these emotional obstacles.

MEET RILEY

Riley, an eighteen-year-old senior in high school, came to see me to work on feeling more socially at ease and comfortable in groups, especially peer groups. Riley had a habit of being overly worried about meeting other people's emotional needs and, in so doing, would abandon his own needs. This contributed to problems with Riley's ability to set aside the time to do what was important to him, like pursuing his hobbies and school. And the word *no* was not a part of his vocabulary. This dynamic made his relationships emotionally exhausting and incredibly difficult. Riley was also getting ready to start college in a few months. He was worried about making new friends, getting along with his roommate, and keeping up with his studies and classes. He didn't want this pattern of interacting to follow him throughout college. He was also particularly concerned that he would not genuinely feel he was a part of his school's larger community. In fact, Riley never felt like he genuinely belonged anywhere. This feeling was longstanding and went back to Riley's early childhood.

Most of Riley's early childhood memories involved watching his father get drunk night after night. Riley described his mother as "a classic codependent."

"My mother denied my father had a drinking problem my whole life!" he told me. "Even when I would confront her about it, she would give an excuse for his drinking like, 'He drinks a little at night because he works so hard' or 'He never got a DUI' and 'Doesn't he deserve some time to unwind after a hard day at work? He rarely gets so drunk that he can't *walk*.'"

Codependency, as we learned earlier, describes a dynamic in which one person enables and supports another person's dysfunctional behavior or poor emotional health, like alcohol or substance abuse, immaturity, irresponsibility, and underachievement. In Riley's case, his mother's codependent behavior led her to deny her husband had a severe drinking problem and to neglect many of her son's emotional and physical needs—not to mention abandon her own needs!

"My parents rarely paid attention to me," Riley continued. "They were so wrapped up in each other in sick and unhealthy ways. I can't remember my mom or dad ever taking an interest in my life. Neither one ever asked me how my classes were going, about my friends, or what interests I had."

Riley also came to realize that he had internalized his mother's codependent behaviors. This was most apparent in his relationships with his friends. Not only was Riley preoccupied with the well-being of his friends, he also actively sought their reassurance. And many of his friends suffered from depression or another mental-health disorder. As for social media, Riley's deep need for reassurance also showed up in his online habits. Riley would regularly agonize over what to post and how to word them. After posting them, he would become consumed with how his friends might respond to his posts and the number of comments he would receive. Riley would spend the next twenty-four hours continually checking his social media accounts and reviewing what he had posted.

CODEPENDENCY, DYSFUNCTIONAL FAMILIES, AND SOCIAL MEDIA

Another core characteristic of codependency is an excessive reliance on other people for approval and a sense of identity.[16] With this in mind, it's not hard to imagine how a person with codependent behaviors and characteristics could develop an unhealthy relationship with social media. In addition to its contributing to issues with social-media use, codependency also inhibits authentic feelings of belonging. This is due to the codependent's enduring struggle with identity, self-concept, and a deep longing to be liked and feel accepted, causing the codependent to take on the personalities of those they are with.

It's important to acknowledge that having dependency needs is healthy and normal. In mature and healthy relationships, people are able to comfortably rely on one another for support, understanding, and help, while at the same time retaining a sense of independence and autonomy. This dynamic is reciprocated, not just one-sided. Healthy dynamics between people foster independence, resourcefulness, and resiliency, while codependent dynamics stifle and limit growth. This is especially true for the codependent; so many of their thinking and behaviors are organized around another's perceived expectations and desires.

BACK TO RILEY

"Social media, for me, has its positives and negatives," Riley shared with me one day in session.

> The negatives are that I get too invested in other people's responses to my posts. Since I'm a lot like Mom, I also seek out emotional reassurance from people. And social media is another arena I use to meet this emotional need of mine. But I know it's unhealthy, because, ultimately, I need to be able to do this for myself.
>
> Another negative thing about social media for me is that it reinforces my feeling like an outsider. Most of my friends use social media to post pictures of themselves with their friends! I get really jealous of other people who have a friend group and post pictures of themselves doing fun things with a group of people. On the other

hand, when I do get the courage to post a status update like, "Just slayed another ten-mile run!" I usually get comments that are pretty positive, like, "Wow!" and "That's Great!" or "Keep it up!"

Comments like this make me feel that people actually care about me. And the reassurance I get from these posts feels positive and healthy. I guess because I feel pretty good about these posts too. And I'm sharing them because I'm feeling genuinely proud of myself. Something I rarely get with my own family. When I get positive and encouraging comments, it also makes me realize that not all people are harmful and that not all relationships are like the ones my parents have with each other or the relationship I have with them.

For Riley, as with Jackie, social media is a space where there's an opportunity to experience corrective emotional experiences. Positive comments from his followers and friends positively impact Riley's sense of self, identity, and well-being. They make him feel cared for, important, and noticed—what we all need to feel in order to grow, develop, and thrive.

I also believed social media could help Riley with his transition from high school to college by increasing his sense of belonging. There's current research linking social media to improving students' adjustment to college as well as their sense of belonging.[17] For example, it's now common practice for universities and colleges to have designated Facebook pages for each class and incoming class, the alumni, their faculty, and online clubs and athletics. Social networking of this kind helps guide students in their adjustment to the unfamiliar social environment at college. As far as social media's contribution to belonging, social-networking sites help students learn about their peers and college, which, in turn, creates affiliation with their university. Students' sense of belonging—that is, whether or not they feel included in their college community—has a documented relationship with college adjustment. For instance, student perceptions of belonging have been positively associated with feelings of social acceptance and academic competence.[18]

In a few months, Riley was going to start college. His college had a Facebook group, which he joined. Together, Riley and I worked to create a profile that truly reflected his identity and interests. Next, Riley and I worked toward helping him expand his networks from individual peers to groups by exploring what clubs he'd be interested in joining once at college. Riley shared that he liked hiking and was excited to learn that his college had a hiking club and that the club had a Facebook page he could join. With some encouragement, Riley posted on the group page, expressing his interest, and he even used a hashtag, which broadened his post's reach. Not surprisingly, Riley got positive responses to his post, encouraging him to join.

SKILL-BUILDING STRATEGY

Fortunately, codependency is a learned behavior and can be changed with treatment. Below are a few ways in which you can begin to change codependent behaviors, both online and off.

- Cultivate awareness. Keep a journal for writing down codependent behaviors you notice in yourself and the situations in which they are most prevalent. For example, when someone appears to be struggling online and offline, do you automatically jump in to help or rescue? Do you help to the extent that your own emotional and physical needs are put on the back burner? Are you preoccupied with other people's problems online and offline to the extent that it interferes with pursuing your own goals and caring for your own needs? Codependent behaviors, in part, are normal feelings of responsibility and compassion gone awry.
- Set healthy boundaries. This is a crucial step in changing codependent behaviors. Being able to say no without feeling guilty, anxious, or afraid is what having healthy boundaries feels like. This is challenging for codependent individuals. Since pleasing others is crucial to their sense of self, saying no is scary and anxiety-inducing. Have a clear understanding of the boundaries that feel right to you, and write them down. Place this list in an area of your home where you can regularly read it. This will help reinforce your boundaries and make them more conscious to you. Be prepared by knowing that upholding your limits will be difficult, at best,

in the beginning. Have a plan in place for coping with these difficult feelings by making sure you're making time to take care of yourself during this transition.

- Find your voice. Feeling entitled to having your own thoughts, feelings, and opinions—even when others do not agree or feel the same way—is essential for breaking codependent behaviors. Online, get more comfortable posting your thoughts and opinions rather than what you believe others want to hear or expect. Codependent behaviors are formed and reinforced by internal pressure to please others, which means that the codependent person, therefore, has not developed their own identity or individuality. Working on developing an authentic sense of self and healthy entitlement increases self-esteem and self-respect, both of which act as a buffer against continuing codependent behaviors.

- Go to therapy. Codependency is a set of behaviors and beliefs about one's self and others that form in early childhood. Talking with a professional offers a better understanding of your unique reasons for developing codependent behaviors. Once your codependent behaviors are fully understood, your chances of developing future codependent relationships are lowered, and your chances of having mutually satisfying and healthy relationships rise.

WHERE TO GO FROM HERE

The need to belong is an innate human drive. We all seek to feel and to be a part of something greater than ourselves—whether an e-tribe, Facebook group, family, peer group, religious community, or professional association. Furthermore, psychologists see belongingness as a remedy to feelings of loneliness and alienation. But for so many, achieving a genuine sense of belonging and affiliation is a lifelong challenge. Issues around attachment, personality disorders, anxiety, or trauma stemming back to our early life are some of the many reasons we may struggle to meet our need for connection and belongingness.

In an era where belonging seems it would be easier to achieve, researchers say we're actually more lonely and disconnected than ever.

Using social media to foster a sense of belonging is not without its limitations and potential adverse side effects, of course. As we've seen, researchers have identified a connection between social-media use and loneliness, lower perceptions of social skills, academic procrastination, social isolation, increased negative thoughts and emotions after a romantic separation, increased opportunity to experience cyberbullying, and reduced academic performance.

But it's not all bad news. There are ways in which social media and various social-networking sites can jump-start otherwise-dormant feelings of belonging. Specifically, social media has been found to facilitate offline social interactions and help us expand our social circles by increasing the sheer numbers of people with whom we interact on a daily basis, to provide corrective emotional experiences, and to deepen the quality of our friendships. While psychological pitfalls associated with social-media use do exist, studies show they can be moderated by decreasing the amount of time we spend online, being clear about our motivation and intentions when using social media, using appropriate privacy settings, and being mindful of the quality of our online friendships established via social media.

Below are five recommendations to help get you started along the path to feeling a more profound sense of belonging.

RECOMMENDATIONS

1. Create an authentic social-media profile that represents your accomplishments and genuine passions, interests, and personal values. The more authentic you are both online and offline, the more open you'll be to experiencing real feelings of connection and belonging. We pay a high price when we aren't attuned to our true selves. For example, we might pursue a profession that doesn't reflect our genuine interests, or we might stay in relationships for too long with people with whom we genuinely don't have much in common.

2. Join an online group. Whether it is a group about cats or a fan group about famous Russian authors, being a part of something greater than yourself, online and offline, is necessary for achieving belongingness.

3. Maximize positive lived shared experiences with those who are important to you, online and offline. Sharing positive experiences and good news deepens bonds and attachments, all of which promotes feelings of belongingness.

4. Say yes to invitations to connect, online and offline. Every invitation is a chance to connect with those around you and therefore maximize your sense of belongingness in the world.

5. Find your authentic voice, online and offline. Our most meaningful connections are with those by whom we feel entirely accepted and understood.

9

BALANCING THE VIRTUAL AND THE ACTUAL LIFE

Happiness depends on ourselves.

—Aristotle[1]

Many people struggle with being able to balance their busy lives. Between work, school, family, and all the other responsibilities that encompass living, adding technology into the mix makes achieving balance even harder.

A recent study by *RescueTime Blog* found that

- We spend three hours and fifteen minutes a day on average on our phones
- The average person checks their phone fifty-eight times a day and
- We rarely go for more than two hours without touching our phones.[2]

Our gadgets have a seductive and enticing quality that makes them hard to ignore, let alone put down! We indulge our curiosity the second we hear the ding from an incoming e-mail or text. Social media pulls us in to see what our friends are doing so we can squash our fear of missing out. The newest news alert pops up on our screen, screaming for our attention. What was once meant to make our lives easier and less complicated is doing the opposite: when logged on, we're more stressed out, more depressed, and more anxious than ever.

Managing our stress and finding balance in the digital age is an essential undertaking for our physical and mental health. We know that Internet overload and too much time spent on social media leads to procrastination, anxiety, depression, malignant envy, FOMO, social comparisons, loneliness, and mental and physical exhaustion. We also know that those who score high on assessments for FOMO, anxiety, depression, social comparisons, anxious attachment, and envy are more likely to overuse technology and social media in ways that undermine their mental health—thus creating a vicious cycle of self-defeating behavior.[3]

There's even reason to believe that our phones and other devices are shortening our lifespans. Evidence shows that just having a phone in the same room as us raises our stress and cortisol levels. Extended periods of high cortisol levels increase our risk for diabetes, depression, insomnia, high blood pressure, cardiac disease, and obesity, among other health issues. There's now a recognized medical condition, text neck, which refers to stress injury and pain in the neck caused by looking down too often and too long at our iPhones, tablets, or other devices.[4]

Technology is here to stay, making it a permanent part of our existence. Throughout this book, we have reviewed numerous studies investigating technology's impact on our emotional health that tell us passive consumption of social media can make us feel worse than we had felt moments before we logged on and that the more time we spend on social media, the worse we will feel! We also know that using social media to meet our attachment needs over in-person interactions also undermines our emotional well-being. The purpose of this chapter in particular and book is to help readers learn to use social media in skillful and effective ways. Technology should enhance our lives, not complicate it. Learning to live a balanced life in the digital age is possible. This chapter gives readers four recommendations to help with integrating technology into your daily life in ways that allow for maximum enjoyment.

RECOMMENDATION #1: PRIORITIZE REAL-LIFE RELATIONSHIPS OVER SCREEN TIME

I hear this kind of thing a lot in my practice:

"I'm so lonely."

"I haven't spoken to my son in five years. I'm just sick over it."

"My wife and I are constantly fighting. And when we're not fighting, we ignore each other."

We all suffer when our significant relationships aren't going well, making it harder to bring balance into our lives. After all, it's thought that our deepest desires center on being loved and being able to love. Most psychologists agree that in order to be happy we need someone to love, something meaningful to do, and things to look forward to.

Good relationships keep us happier and healthier, says Robert Waldinger, psychiatrist and psychoanalyst and director of the Harvard Study of Adult Development. Furthermore, it's not the number of friends we have that makes us happier; rather, it's the quality of our relationships.[5] To date, the Harvard study is the most comprehensive study on emotional well-being in history. Supporting John Bowlby's groundbreaking theories on the benefits of secure attachment, Waldinger's research links having warm and secure relationships in childhood to better outcomes in our health and emotional well-being in our later years. In fact, there's a link between the presence of meaningful relationships and heart health—all good reasons for prioritizing our in-person relationships!

Couples or individuals who come to me for help improving their relationships frequently ask, "Where do I start? Where do we start?" "What can we do to change things now?" One thing I tell people they can do right away to improve their relationships is to prioritize their real-life relationships over time on screens by unplugging when with others. In fact, you could even make this a golden rule for yourself, and, if you're feeling empowered, you can ask those you're with to do the same. You can back up your request with the knowledge you've gained by reading this book. For instance, we now know the importance of shared experiences and that sharing lived experiences with our friends and family deepens our attachments and builds memories. With this in mind, sharing real-life experiences while answering texts, responding to e-mails, or posting on social media is counterproductive.

Finally, lots of articles have been written about the phenomenon *phubbing*—the act of looking at your iPhone while in the physical presence of another.[6] I'm sure it's safe to say that most of us have firsthand experience of phubbing: while in the middle of a conversation, the person you're talking to suddenly diverts their attention to look at their iPhone; or perhaps you were the culprit—the one who looked at their phone while someone else was in the middle of expressing themselves to you.

Although phubbing might sound inconsequential, phubbing shows us how technology diminishes our social interactions rather than enhancing them. A recent study examining the psychological drives behind phubbing—such as Internet addiction, FOMO, poor self-control, and smartphone addiction—found that those individuals scoring high on assessments for Internet addiction, FOMO, and low self-control or frustration tolerance tended to phub more. In other words, those that frequently looked at their iPhone when in the presence of another person struggled with FOMO, had low levels of self-control, and overused technology. Furthermore, phubbing is likely to be a symptom of digital overuse. And digital overuse erodes our real-life relationships.

Building warm and secure relationships takes work—just like anything else worth having in life. It's important to understand that having relationships doesn't mean your relationship will be perfect and without conflict. It means that you'll be more skillfully able to work out conflicts in ways that deepen bonds rather than dissolve them. But the truth of the matter is that, for many, and for a multitude of reasons, having secure relationships is difficult. For example, someone who grew up in a dysfunctional family and never learned how to have close and trusting relationships may push people away or do and say hurtful things to prevent closeness. And others may use technology or social media as a stand-in for intimacy and in place of intimate relationships.

If this sounds like you, talking to a professional can help you figure out how your screen use is stopping you from developing healthier relationships. Although asking for help can be more difficult for some of us than it is for others, being able to acknowledge that we need help can improve our relationships. When we share our burdens, we create intimacy, and we know that intimacy leads to more satisfying relationships.

When we ask for help, we communicate to others that while we may not have all the answers, we are willing to seek them out and find solutions to our problems, which creates an atmosphere of empowerment. It connects us to other people by making us realize that we are not alone in our struggles. Ultimately, we grow emotionally when we gain the ability to ask for help.

SKILL-BUILDING STRATEGIES

Below are a few tips to help you balance virtual relationships and real-life relationships.

- Ask yourself why you are using social-networking sites. Is it to build relationships, for professional-networking purposes, to connect to old friends, or to stay connected to those that live far away? Once you determine what you are looking for, you can set realistic goals.
- Limit your time on social-networking sites. This will help control the amount of time you are spending online.
- Make sure to include texts or private messages in your repertoire of computer-mediated communications. If social-networking sites cause you to feel disconnected, depressed, or lonely, consider upping your interactions with people by sending them a private message or even a text message. This level of virtual communication is more personal and intimate than communicating in an open forum.
- Make sure to schedule time to see your friends and family beyond the virtual world. As we're learning, having positive, secure relationships is strongly associated with high levels of self-esteem and resilience. Relationships of this kind foster feelings of connectedness and decrease our risk for depression and anxiety.

RECOMMENDATION #2: SET VIRTUAL BOUNDARIES

Does any of this sound familiar?

"I feel guilty if I don't immediately respond to someone on social media instead of doing my work, even though I know it will distract me!"

"It takes me longer to get the simplest tasks done because I take so many tech breaks to check e-mails, read the news, or play Candy

Crush instead of just powering through and getting my important work done!"

"I'm finding it harder and harder to start my day off feeling positive after I've been on social media."

"I never had issues with procrastination until I joined Facebook."

Many studies link Internet and social-network use to procrastination, lower academic achievement, and poorer concentration.[7] One such study found that those with low self-control, habitual Facebook checking, and high enjoyment of Facebook are the very ones most likely to use Facebook as a form of procrastination. Moreover, it's not surprising that this study also found that using Facebook to avoid attending to important tasks contributes to elevated stress levels and negatively affects well-being.

In another study, researchers found that watching YouTube videos of cats instead of doing more important tasks resulted in feelings of guilt, thereby decreasing enjoyment derived from the YouTube viewing. The prevalence of using technology and social media as a means for procrastination is increasing, alongside the ever-increasing number of digital options now available for avoiding work and other responsibilities. It's no surprise to learn that setting firm boundaries around your technology use is key to preventing the vicious cycle of using technology in unhealthy ways.

But for many, setting limits and boundaries around their use of technology can be just as hard as setting boundaries in their interpersonal relationships. As I mentioned earlier in this book, boundaries communicate the rules and limits to those around us regarding the type of treatment we expect from others and what others can expect from us. For example, our boundaries communicate, "This is how far I shall go." "This is what I will or won't do for you." "This is what I won't accept or tolerate from you." Someone's personal boundary might be that no one can enter their bedroom without asking permission or that jokes and sarcastic comments about weight or appearance are off-limits.

Boundary setting is a skill we learn in childhood; but those raised in dysfunctional families might have a hard time identifying the difference between healthy and unhealthy boundaries and then have an even harder time implementing them. If you fall into this category, take the time to ask yourself, "What are my actual limits?" and "Are there boundaries I can set that will make my life easier and better?" You might even consider getting help from a mental-health professional as you begin learning what healthy boundaries are and how to set appropriate limits. We all need boundaries. Taking the time and energy to set them is worth it. Ultimately, healthy boundaries will provide you with more time and skills for living a balanced life in the digital age.

Having designated tech-free spaces in our environments or home is also important for implementing boundaries around technology. In fact, there's research to back up the benefits of having our bedrooms be tech-free. For instance, studies show a correlation between sleep issues, such as insomnia, with screen time. The blue light from our cell phones, laptops, and other devices disrupts our circadian rhythm, leading to issues with sleep-wake cycles and poor sleep hygiene, which, in turn, can lead to a host of health issues.[8] In my professional experience, those who have set up virtual boundaries in their homes or other spaces they frequent report lower levels of anxiety and depression and report noticeable improvements in focus, concentration, memory, and relationships.

SKILL-BUILDING STRATEGIES

Below are some suggestions to help you with setting boundaries.

- Learn to say no. Many of us have a hard time saying no when asked to give our time or energy, but overextending ourselves doesn't help anyone in the long run. Practice taking a moment to think through requests for help instead of immediately taking them on as your own burden. You can buy yourself time to thoughtfully consider your answer first by saying something like, "I'll check my calendar and circle back with you later."
- List all the reasons why setting firm boundaries around technology will help you. For example, ask yourself, "Why is it important that I turn off my iPhone when I'm working on an important project?" Or "Why is putting my iPhone in another room helping me relax?" Knowing why we are doing something helps us figure out how to do it.

RECOMMENDATION #3: STRENGTHEN YOUR FRUSTRATION TOLERANCE

Do any of the following statements ring true for you?

"I can't stand not having my iPhone with me!"

"I must check my social-media accounts so I know what my friends are up to!"

"I should always be available to my mother, father, son, daughter, partner, friend, or boss."

"I feel afraid when I don't have my phone."

According to Aristotle, happiness is found when we perfect our human nature and enrich our lives through finding a balance of health, wealth, knowledge, and friends throughout our entire lives. Life requires that we make choices, often meaning we have to sacrifice our desire for "instant gratification." *Frustration tolerance*—our ability to withstand the discomfort of frustration—is a necessary skill that helps us find balance. For example, of course it's easier to log on to social media or sit on the couch and stream Netflix rather than face the day's long list of responsibilities, such as caring for an elderly parent, cleaning the house, cooking dinner, finishing a work project, or working on a term paper. It is obvious that indulging our wishes in this way for an extended period of time causes us more harm than good. There's a *big* difference, however, between knowing this to be true and doing something to change our behavior.

For many, the significant distress that arises from just the thought of not having their iPhone, even for a short amount of time, is based on the belief that they would be unable to tolerate any amount of deprivation. In short, irrational beliefs such as, "I'll die without my iPhone" or "I must immediately respond to my friends' texts" or "I literally can't stand being offline," combined with low frustration tolerance lead to imbalances between our virtual and actual lives.

Developing a healthy degree of frustration tolerance is not only necessary for finding balance in the digital age, it's also an essential component of successful treatment and optimal emotional health. Frustration tolerance is dependent upon each of our ego strength and personal agency. To begin with, ego strength is determined by aspects of our personality, attitude, or behavior that helps us maintain good mental health in the face of adversity or painful experiences. In ego psychology, *ego strength* is defined as the capacity of the ego to cope with conflicting demands of the id, superego, and reality. In treatment, identifying a person's ego strength is a vital determinant of how well they will cope with painful life situations.

Optimal frustration tolerance, a term associated with self-psychology, specifically refers to the ability to manage feelings of frustration in ways that lead to emotional growth and to the development of new coping skills.[9] For example, rather than reaching for your iPhone when you feel frustrated while in the middle of completing a task, take a few deep breaths and tell yourself, "I can stand it" and "I will survive not looking at my iPhone at this very moment." Deep-breathing exercises and the use of self-affirming statements to decrease anxiety strengthen our frustration tolerance and go a long way toward helping us resist overindulging in behaviors such as mindlessly playing Candy Crush or going on social media—behaviors that ultimately lead to more frustration, depression, anxiety, and guilt.

Learning how to move from "the knowing zone" into the "doing zone" is key to finding balance and making healthy decisions in the digital age. Most psychologists believe our sense of personal agency is what's responsible for allowing us to take action in our lives.

Personal agency refers to our ability to create and to direct actions for given purposes. Like taking the action to work on a term paper instead of watching Netflix or going for a run instead of eating a carton of cookies, having healthy relationships requires a sense of personal agency, such as talking about your feelings to a friend instead of turning to social media for a feeling of connectedness. In a nutshell, when we have a sense of agency, we're able to take action.

It's not hard to see how developing both frustration tolerance and personal agency is essential for gaining balance in the digital age. Just like building up our body's muscles, strengthening frustration tolerance takes practice, dedication, time, and energy.

SKILL-BUILDING STRATEGIES

Devoting time to strengthening frustration tolerance can enable us to resist negative social-media and technology habits and get started or stick with other activities that will bring us a feeling of accomplishment or joy. Most goals require that we tolerate frustration. Below are a few tips to help you build frustration tolerance and gain balance in the digital age.

- Accept your feelings of frustration. Frustration is a normal human emotion and reaction to life's unpredictability. It might sound counterintuitive, but the more we fight feelings of frustration, the longer those feelings will linger.
- Ride it out. Work on being able to ride out feelings of frustration and other negative emotions. Accept that problems are a part of life. Acceptance means knowing our feelings are cyclical and that sometimes the only way through is to ride out the uncomfortable emotions. Being able to "sit with" negative feelings rather than impulsively react is also helpful for finding effective solutions to the issue that created our frustration in the first place. It's difficult for most people to come up with effective solutions when feeling emotionally overwhelmed.
- Revisit lessons from past frustrations. Many people underestimate their ability to tolerate frustrating circumstances. Recall difficult experiences from the past that you tolerated, and explore how you endured them. Ask yourself, "What did I tell myself that helped me complete these tasks?" Find ways to question the validity of your frustration and reframe your negative thinking. For example, "I was able to stand this in the past; I'll be able to stand it again."
- Practice mindfulness. Anxiety makes it harder to cultivate frustration tolerance, because when we're tense, our bodies and our minds are wound up. Mindfulness helps us slow down our mind and body, which is key for learning to tolerate frustration. Some ways to practice mindfulness are to do

deep-breathing exercises, be in the present moment, or use imagery. For example, imagine yourself lying in a peaceful meadow or on a beach. You can also download an imagery app to help you.

RECOMMENDATION #4: COMMIT TO NONDIGITAL SELF-CARE PRACTICES

What's self-care? Simply put, *self-care* is the intentional act of taking time to pay attention to you. I don't mean in a narcissistic way, which leaves us feeling exhausted and empty; I'm referring to the type of self-care that lifts, energizes, and recharges us. Research supports that making self-care a priority leads to greater work-life-technology balance.[10] In my practice, I often find that a lack of self-care is a crucial, underlying issue in those struggling with technology and social-media overuse. When we neglect our self-care, we are more vulnerable to feeling stressed-out, depressed, and anxious. We're also more likely to abuse substances, overuse technology, and have a lower sense of personal agency.

I believe a good way to find balance in the digital era—in addition to making sure we exercise, eat a healthy diet rich in fruits and vegetables, and get the recommended seven to eight hours of sleep a night—is to tend to our emotional, spiritual, and cognitive needs. One excellent self-care practice is making time to connect with nature. In our digital age, being outside and spending time in natural settings is becoming more and more of a luxury. But studies are showing that time away from natural settings is taking a toll on our emotional and physical health.

In fact, the growing scientific field of ecotherapy has shown a strong connection between time spent in nature and reduced stress, anxiety, and depression. One recent study compared the brain activity of healthy people after they walked for ninety minutes in either a natural setting or an urban one. Their results showed that nature walks lower activity in the prefrontal cortex, a brain region that is active during *rumination*—which is defined as repetitive thoughts that focus on negative emotions.[11] If you're short on time or live in an urban area with few natural settings, try listening to calming nature sounds, like birds or forest creek sounds. Research shows that these activities can lower blood pressure and levels of cortisol, calming the body's fight-or-flight response.

Another important self-care practice for finding balance in the digital age is to work on developing hobbies and interests outside of professional and family commitments. Find enjoyable activities that don't involve technology—like painting, drawing, reading, volunteering, exercise, and travel—and that produce feelings of flow or like you're "in the zone." The state of *flow* or feeling like you're in the zone happens when we're fully immersed in activities that we enjoy. In short, flow is characterized by the complete absorption in what we are doing, resulting in loss of our sense of space and time. [12]

Another reason for pursuing nonvirtual interests and activities that put us in a state of flow is that most of them are also good for our cognitive and emotional development. For example, a recent study with mice and humans found that brainy activities stimulate new connections between nerve cells and may even help the brain generate new ones, developing neurological "plasticity" and building up a functional reserve that provides a hedge against future cell loss. Essentially, mentally stimulating activity helps to build up our brains. Activities like reading, word puzzles, painting, and drawing not only put us in a state of flow, they're also good for our brain health. [13]

SKILL-BUILDING STRATEGIES

Below are five essential self-care tips to get you on your way to a happier and healthier you.

- Take care of your physical needs by getting plenty of sleep, regular exercise, and eating a balanced diet. Research has consistently shown these practices to significantly improve our concentration and cognition and to lessen depression and anxiety.
- Tune in to your emotions. Developing the ability to recognize and label our emotions is a necessary skill for cultivating our well-being. All too often, we are distracted by our busy lives and rarely have an opportunity to take a moment for

self-reflection. Schedule regular times for self-reflection by writing in a journal or meditating. Before you log on to social media, get in the habit of checking in with yourself. For example, if you're feeling more stressed or blue, it's probably best to skip social media for a little while.

- Make your self-care a priority. Honoring the commitments we make to ourselves reinforces the notion that we matter.

- Create your own self-care rituals. Take time to define what self-care rituals are important to you and how to implement them in your day. For example, for some people, making time for silence and solitude may be at the top of their self-care list, while for others socializing with friends is most important.

- Be mindful of how and with whom you spend your time. The activities we choose to do and the people we choose to share our lives with are reflections of how we feel about ourselves. As often as you can, schedule time to do the things you enjoy with people you enjoy and love!

WRAP-UP

For some of us, finding balance in the digital age may seem impossible. Life is a journey, not a destination. It's normal to sometimes feel like we're on the wrong path. It is during these times that we're more likely to question our decisions, our feelings, our relationships, and our past and be fearful about our future.

Change of every kind starts with awareness, acceptance, and action. For most of us, this means doing things differently. If your social-media use is making it harder to find your footing again when you feel off-balance, or if it's making your life more complicated than it needs to be, take the time to practice the skill-building strategies I've offered throughout this book. You can start with choosing one behavior to work on until you feel comfortable enough to start on another one. It's important to know that if you're struggling with improving your screen health and overall emotional health, you should consider talking to a mental-health professional. Talking can help get you to a place of awareness, acceptance, and action. Most of all, remember to be patient with yourself. Change takes time. That's just life. There are no simple solutions to complex problems, even if social media tries to make us believe otherwise.

Good luck on your journey to finding balance in the digital age!

NOTES

INTRODUCTION

1. Philippe Verduyn et al., "Passive Facebook Usage Undermines Affective Well-Being: Experimental and Longitudinal Evidence," *Journal of Experimental Psychology: General* 144, no. 2 (2015): 480–88, doi:10.1037/xge0000057.

2. Neil Petersen, "How Social Media Influences Offline Behavior," *AllPsych* (blog), March 31, 2017, https://blog.allpsych.com/how-social-media-influences-offline-behavior/.

3. Pew Research Center, "Social Media Fact Sheet," Internet & Technology, June 12, 2019, https://www.pewresearch.org/internet/fact-sheet/social-media/.

4. Attributed to Sigmund Freud.

I. BUILDING RELATIONSHIPS IN THE DIGITAL AGE

1. Sigmund Freud to his fiancée, Martha Bernays, June 27, 1882, in *Letters of Sigmund Freud, 1873–1939*, ed. Ernst L. Freud, trans. Tania Stern and James Stern (London: Hogarth Press, 1960, 1961), 28.

2. Harvard Health Publishing, "Can Relationships Boost Longevity and Well-being?" *Harvard Health Letter*, last modified September 24, 2019, https://webcache.googleusercontent.com/search?q=cache:h126n1Jd7FYJ:https://www.health.harvard.edu/mental-health/can-relationships-boost-longevity-and-well-being+&cd=1&hl=en&ct=clnk&gl=us&client=safari.

3. Attributed to Lucius Annaeus Seneca.

4. Shoba Sreenivasan and Linda E. Weinberger, "Why We Need Each Other," *Psychology Today*, December 14, 2016, https://www.psychologytoday.com/us/blog/emotional-nourishment/201612/why-we-need-each-other.

5. Abraham H. Maslow, "A Theory of Human Motivation," *Psychological Review* 50 (1943): 370–96, text available at http://psychclassics.yorku.ca/Maslow/motivation.htm.

6. Erik H. Erikson, *Childhood and Society* (New York: W. W. Norton & Company, 1950).

7. "Relational Therapy," *Psychology Today*, accessed January 20, 2020, https://www.psychologytoday.com/us/therapy-types/relational-therapy.

8. Vaughn G. Sinclair and Sharon W. Dowdy, "Development and Validation of the Emotional Intimacy Scale," *Journal of Nursing Measurement* 13, no. 3 (2005): 193–206, doi:10.1891/jnum.13.3.193.

9. Gabriel Marcel, *The Philosophy of Existence*, trans. Manya Harari (London: The Harvill Press), 25.

10. Sherry Turkle, *Alone Together: Why We Expect More from Technology and Less from Each Other* (New York: Basic Books, 2017).

11. Cristina Miguel Martos, "The Transformation of Intimacy and Privacy through Social Networking Sites," paper, accessed January 27, 2020, available online at http://pvac-webhost2.leeds.ac.uk/ics/files/2013/07/Miguel_The-Transformation-of-Intimacy-and-Privacy-through-Social-Networking-Sites.pdf.

12. Stephanie A. Sarkis, "11 Warning Signs of Gaslighting," *Psychology Today*, January 22, 2017, https://www.psychologytoday.com/us/blog/here-there-and-everywhere/201701/11-warning-signs-gaslighting.

13. Cristina Miguel, "Visual Intimacy on Social Media: From Selfies to the Co-construction of Intimacies through Shared Pictures," *Social Media + Society* 2, no. 2 (2016): 205630511664170, doi:10.1177/2056305116641705, https://journals.sagepub.com/doi/10.1177/2056305116641705.

14. Richard L. Daft and Robert H. Lengel, "Organizational Information Requirements, Media Richness and Structural Design," *Management Science* 32, no. 5 (1986): 554–71, doi:10.1287/mnsc.32.5.554.

15. Maria C. D'Arienzo, Valentina Boursier, and Mark D. Griffiths, "Addiction to Social Media and Attachment Styles: A Systematic Literature Review," *International Journal of Mental Health and Addiction* 17, no. 4 (2019): 1094–18, doi:10.1007/s11469-019-00082-5.

2. SCREEN ATTACHMENTS

1. Attributed to John Bowlby. In 2005 Bowlby wrote, "All of us, from the cradle to the grave, are happiest when life is organized as a series of excursions, long or short, from the secure base provided by our attachment figure(s)." John Bowlby, *A Secure Base: Clinical Applications of Attachment Theory* (London: Routledge, 2005), 69.

2. Deloitte, *2018 Global Mobile Consumer Survey: US Edition; A New Era in Mobile Continues* (New York: Deloitte Development, LLC, 2018), https://www2.deloitte.com/content/dam/Deloitte/us/Documents/technology-media-telecommunications/us-tmt-global-mobile-consumer-survey-exec-summary-2018.pdf.

3. Vanessa M. Buote, Eileen Wood, and Michael Pratt, "Exploring Similarities and Differences between Online and Offline Friendships: The Role of Attachment Style," *Computers in Human Behavior* 25, no. 2 (2009): 560–67, https://doi.org/10.1016/j.chb.2008.12.022.

4. John Bowlby, *Attachment and Loss*, vol. 1, *Attachment* (New York: Basic Books, 1969); John Bowlby, *Attachment and Loss*, vol. 2, *Separation: Anxiety and Anger* (New York: Basic Books, 1973); John Bowlby, *Attachment and Loss*, vol. 3, *Loss* (New York: Basic Books, 1980).

5. Mary D. Salter Ainsworth et al., *Patterns of Attachment: A Psychological Study of the Strange Situation* (Hillsdale, NJ: Erlbaum, 1978).

6. Pew Research Center, "Social Media Fact Sheet."

7. D'Arienzo, Boursier, and Griffiths, "Addiction to Social Media."

8. Terry E. Carrilio and Carolyn A. Walter, "Mirroring and Autonomy: The Dual Tasks of Mothers," *Child & Adolescent Social Work Journal* 1, no. 3 (1984): 143–52, doi:10.1007/bf00798430.

9. Julian A. Oldmeadow, Sally Quinn, and Rachel Kowert, "Attachment Style, Social Skills, and Facebook Use amongst Adults," *Computers in Human Behavior* 29, no. 3 (2013): 1142–49, doi: 10.1016/j.chb.2012.10.006.

3. THE DISTORTED MIRROR

1. Leon Festinger, "A Theory of Social Comparison Processes," *Human Relations* 7, no. 2 (1954): 117–40, doi:10.1177/001872675400700202.

2. Susan T. Fiske, "Envy Up, Scorn Down: How Comparison Divides Us," *American Psychologist* 65, no. 8 (2010): 698–706, doi:10.1037/0003-066x.65.8.698.

3. Ibid.

4. Ibid.

5. Elizabeth L. Auchincloss, Eslee Samberg, and the American Psychoanalytic Association, *Psychoanalytic Terms and Concepts* (New Haven, CT: Yale University Press, 2012).

6. Melanie Klein, *The Writings of Melanie Klein*, vol. 3, *Envy and Gratitude and Other Works, 1946–1963* (London: Hogarth Press, 1975), 201–3.

7. Robert A. Emmons, *Thanks: How Practicing Gratitude Can Make You Happier* (Boston: Houghton Mifflin Harcourt, 2008).

8. Volkan Dogan, "Why Do People Experience the Fear of Missing Out (FoMO)? Exposing the Link between the Self and the FoMO through Self-Construal," *Journal of Cross-Cultural Psychology* 50, no. 4 (2019): 524–38, doi:10.1177/0022022119839145.

9. John M. Grohol, "15 Common Cognitive Distortions," *Psych Central*, last updated June 24, 2019, https://psychcentral.com/lib/15-common-cognitive-distortions/.

10. Christopher Bergland, "Face-to-Face Social Contact Reduces Risk of Depression," *Psychology Today*, October 5, 2015, https://www.psychologytoday.com/us/blog/the-athletes-way/201510/face-face-social-contact-reduces-risk-depression.

4. SUBSTANCE ABUSE, DEPRESSION, BODY IMAGE, AND THE IMPORTANCE OF SOCIAL MEDIA LITERACY

1. Viktor E. Frankl, *Man's Search for Meaning: An Introduction to Logotherapy*, 4th ed., pref. Gordon W. Allport (Boston: Beacon Press, 1992), 116.

2. Andrea Petersen, "As Suicides Rise, More Attention Turns to the People Left Behind," *Wall Street Journal*, December 2, 2019, https://www.wsj.com/articles/as-suicides-rise-more-attention-turns-to-the-people-left-behind-11575282602 (paywall).

3. Wikipedia, s.v. "Media Literacy," last modified March 9, 2020, https://en.wikipedia.org/wiki/Media_literacy.

4. US National Library of Medicine, "Mental Health," *MedlinePlus*, last modified December 3, 2019, https://medlineplus.gov/mentalhealth.html.

5. Jonaki Bose et al., *Key Substance Use and Mental Health Indicators in the United States: Results from the 2017 National Survey on Drug Use and Health*, HHS Publication No. SMA 18-5068, NSDUH Series H-53 (Rockville, MD: Center for Behavioral Health Statistics and Quality, Substance Abuse and Mental Health Services Administration, 2018), https://www.samhsa.gov/data/sites/default/files/cbhsq-reports/NSDUHFFR2017/NSDUHFFR2017.htm; Rachel N. Lipari, Eunice Park-Le, and Substance Abuse and Mental Health

Services Administration (SAMHSA), *Key Substance Use and Mental Health Indicators in the United States: Results from the 2018 National Survey on Drug Use and Health*, HHS publication no. PEP19-5068, NSDUH Series H-54 (Rockville, MD: Center for Behavioral Health Statistics and Quality, Substance Abuse and Mental Health Services Administration, 2019), https://www.samhsa.gov/data/sites/default/files/cbhsq-reports/NSDUHNationalFindingsReport2018/NSDUHNationalFindingsReport2018.pdf.

6. Nicholas Weiler, "Protein Links Alcohol Abuse and Changes in Brain's Reward Center," UC San Francisco, September 7, 2017, https://www.ucsf.edu/news/2017/09/408236/protein-links-alcohol-abuse-and-changes-brains-reward-center.

7. Joseph O'Connor and Andrea Lages, "Thinking about Change: Neuroplasticity," in *Coaching the Brain: Practical Applications of Neuroscience to Coaching* (London: Routledge, 2019), 17–29, doi:10.4324/9780203733370-3.

8. "Facts about Eating Disorders: What the Research Shows," Eating Disorders Coalition, accessed January 29, 2020, http://eatingdisorderscoalition.org.s208556.gridserver.com/couch/uploads/file/fact-sheet_2016.pdf.

9. Richard M. Perloff, "Social Media Effects on Young Women's Body Image Concerns: Theoretical Perspectives and an Agenda for Research," *Sex Roles* 71, nos. 11–12 (2014): 363–77, doi:10.1007/s11199-014-0384-6, https://www.researchgate.net/publication/271740741_Social_Media_Effects_on_Young_Women's_Body_Image_Concerns_Theoretical_Perspectives_and_an_Agenda_for_Research.

10. J. Kevin Thompson and Eric Stice, "Thin-Ideal Internalization: Mounting Evidence for a New Risk Factor for Body-Image Disturbance and Eating Pathology," *Current Directions in Psychological Science* 10, no. 5 (2001): 181–83, doi:10.1111/1467-8721.00144.

11. Patricia van den Berg et al., "The Tripartite Influence Model of Body Image and Eating Disturbance," *Journal of Psychosomatic Research* 53, no. 5 (2002): 1007–20, doi:10.1016/s0022-3999(02)00499-3; Auchincloss, Samberg, and the American Psychoanalytic Association, *Psychoanalytic Terms and Concepts*.

12. Festinger, "A Theory of Social Comparison Processes."

13. Jasmine Fardouly and Lenny R. Vartanian, "Negative Comparisons about One's Appearance Mediate the Relationship between Facebook Usage and Body Image Concerns," *Body Image* 12 (2015): 82–88, doi:10.1016/j.bodyim.2014.10.004.

14. Marsha M. Linehan, *Cognitive-Behavioral Treatment of Borderline Personality Disorder* (New York: Guilford Publications, 2018).

15. Liu Yi Lin et al., "Association between Social Media Use and Depression among U.S. Young Adults," *Depression and Anxiety* 33, no. 4 (2016):

323–31, doi:10.1002/da.22466, https://www.ncbi.nlm.nih.gov/pmc/articles/
PMC4853817/.

5. BREAKING UP IN THE DIGITAL AGE

1. Bowlby, *A Secure Base*, 172.

2. Elisabeth Kübler-Ross and David Kessler, *On Grief and Grieving: Finding the Meaning of Grief through the Five Stages of Loss* (New York: Simon & Schuster, 2005).

3. Deborah Khoshaba, "About Complicated Bereavement Disorder," *Psychology Today*, September 28, 2013, https://www.psychologytoday.com/us/blog/get-hardy/201309/about-complicated-bereavement-disorder-0.

4. American Psychological Association, "APA's Survey Finds Constantly Checking Electronic Devices Linked to Significant Stress for Most Americans," February 23, 2017, https://www.apa.org/news/press/releases/2017/02/checking-devices.

5. American Psychological Association, "Connected and Content: Managing Healthy Technology Use," APA.org, 2017, https://www.apa.org/helpcenter/connected-content.

6. Nick Zagorski, "Using Many Social Media Platforms Linked with Depression, Anxiety Risk," *Psychiatric News* 52, no. 2 (2017): 1, doi:10.1176/appi.pn.2017.1b16, https://psychnews.psychiatryonline.org/doi/full/10.1176/appi.pn.2017.1b16.

7. Verduyn et al., "Passive Facebook Usage."

6. MEDICATING WITH TECHNOLOGY

1. Edith Wharton, "Vesalius in Zante. (1564)," *North American Review* 175, no. 552 (Nov. 1902): 631, text available at https://public.wsu.edu/~campbelld/wharton/whartpoe2.htm#Vesalius%20in%20Zante.%20(1564).

2. Nielsen, "Time Flies: U.S. Adults Now Spend Nearly Half a Day Interacting with Media," July 31, 2018, https://www.nielsen.com/us/en/insights/article/2018/time-flies-us-adults-now-spend-nearly-half-a-day-interacting-with-media/.

3. Regina J. J. M. van den Eijnden, Jeroen S. Lemmens, and Patti M. Valkenburg, "The Social Media Disorder Scale," *Computers in Human Behavior* 61 (2016): 478–87, doi:10.1016/j.chb.2016.03.038, https://www.sciencedirect.com/science/article/pii/S0747563216302059.

4. Alexander Johannes Aloysius Maria van Deursen and Petrus A. M. Kommers, "Modeling Habitual and Addictive Smartphone Behavior: The Role of Smartphone Usage Types, Emotional Intelligence, Social Stress, Self-Regulation, Age, and Gender," *Computers in Human Behavior* 45 (2015): 411–20, doi:10.1016/j.chb.2014.12.039.

5. Michael Akers and Grover Porter, "What Is Emotional Intelligence (EQ)?" *Psych Central*, last modified October 8, 2018, https://psychcentral.com/lib/what-is-emotional-intelligence-eq/.

6. Annelies Verheugt-Pleiter and Margit Deben-Mager, "Transference-Focused Psychotherapy and Mentalization-Based Treatment: Brother and Sister?" *Psychoanalytic Psychotherapy* 20, no. 4 (2006): 297–315, doi:10.1080/02668730601020374.

7. Nina Savelle-Rocklin and Salman Akhtar, *Beyond the Primal Addiction: Food, Sex, Gambling, Internet, Shopping, and Work* (London: Routledge, 2019).

8. Pederson, *The DBT Deck for Clients and Therapists.*

9. Ibid.

7. A CALL FOR SELF-COMPASSION IN THE DIGITAL AGE

1. This oft-repeated quotation attributed to the Dalai Lama derives from his reflections in *The Art of Happiness*: "So, first, if we look at the very pattern of our existence from an early age until our death, we can see the way in which we are fundamentally nurtured by other's affection. It begins at birth. Our very first act after birth is to suck our mother's or someone else's milk. That is an act of affection, of compassion. Without that act, we cannot survive." Dalai Lama XIV and Howard C. Cutler, *The Art of Happiness: A Handbook for Living* (Norwalk, CT: Easton Press, 1998).

2. Juliana G. Breines and Serena Chen, "Self-Compassion Increases Self-Improvement Motivation," *Personality and Social Psychology Bulletin* 38, no. 9 (2012): 1133–43, doi:10.1177/0146167212445599.

3. Christopher K. Germer and Kristin D. Neff, "Self-Compassion in Clinical Practice," *Journal of Clinical Psychology* 69, no. 8 (2013): 856–67, doi:10.1002/jclp.22021.

4. Kristin Neff, "Definition of Self-Compassion," *Self-Compassion*, last modified March 22, 2011, https://self-compassion.org/the-three-elements-of-self-compassion-2.

5. Auchincloss, Samberg, and the American Psychoanalytic Association, *Psychoanalytic Terms and Concepts.*

6. American Psychological Association, "What Is Cognitive Behavioral Therapy?" Clinical Practice Guideline for the Treatment of Posttraumatic Stress Disorder, APA.org, accessed January 29, 2020, https://www.apa.org/ptsd-guideline/patients-and-families/cognitive-behavioral.

7. Paul Gilbert and Chris Irons, "Compassion Focused Therapy," in *The Beginner's Guide to Counselling & Psychotherapy*, ed. Stephen Palmer (London: Routledge, 2015), 127–39.

8. Sara Santarossa and Sarah J. Woodruff, "#SocialMedia: Exploring the Relationship of Social Networking Sites on Body Image, Self-Esteem, and Eating Disorders," *Social Media + Society* 3, no. 2 (2017): 205630511770440, doi:10.1177/2056305117704407, https://journals.sagepub.com/doi/full/10.1177/2056305117704407.

9. Neff, "Definition of Self-Compassion."

10. Robert Lemieux, Sean Lajoie, and Nathan E. Trainor, "Affinity-Seeking, Social Loneliness, and Social Avoidance among Facebook Users," *Psychological Reports* 112, no. 2 (2013): 545–52, doi:10.2466/07.pr0.112.2.545-552.

11. Auchincloss, Samberg, and the American Psychoanalytic Association, *Psychoanalytic Terms and Concepts*.

12. Ibid.

13. Tolstoy's exact words were,

> There can be only one permanent revolution—a moral one; the regeneration of the inner man.
> How is this revolution to take place? Nobody knows how it will take place in humanity, but every man feels it clearly in himself. And yet in our world everybody thinks of changing humanity, and nobody thinks of changing himself.

Leo Tolstoy, "Some Social Remedies: Three Methods of Reform," in *Pamphlets* (Christchurch, Hants.: The Free Age Press, 1900).

8. FINDING YOUR E-TRIBE

1. Jane Howard, *Families* (New York: Simon & Schuster, 1978).

2. Julianne Holt-Lunstad, Timothy B. Smith, and J. B. Layton, "Social Relationships and Mortality Risk: A Meta-analytic Review," *PLoS Medicine* 7, no. 7 (2010): e1000316, doi:10.1371/journal.pmed.1000316, https://journals.plos.org/plosmedicine/article?id=10.1371/journal.pmed.1000316.

3. Helen Keller reportedly repeated this sentiment while on a touring circuit with Anne Sullivan, the governess and companion who had taught Keller as a young girl, blind and deaf from a childhood illness, to communicate by spelling words into her hand. From Joseph P. Lash, *Helen and Teacher: The Story of Helen Keller and Anne Sullivan Macy* (New York: Delacorte Press/ Seymour Lawrence, New York, 1980), 489.

4. Roy F. Baumeister and Mark R. Leary, "The Need to Belong: Desire for Interpersonal Attachments as a Fundamental Human Motivation," *Psychological Bulletin* 117, no. 3 (1995): 497–529, doi:10.1037/0033-2909.117.3.497.

5. Abraham H. Maslow, *Motivation and Personality*, 2nd ed. (New York: Aesculapius, 1970).

6. Virginia M. Shiller, *The Attachment Bond: Affectional Ties across the Lifespan* (Lanham, MD: Lexington Books, 2017).

7. Zelda G. Knight, "The Use of the 'Corrective Emotional Experience' and the Search for the Bad Object in Psychotherapy," *American Journal of Psychotherapy* 59, no. 1 (2005): 30–41, doi:10.1176/ appi.psychotherapy.2005.59.1.30.

8. John A. Naslund et al., "The Future of Mental Health Care: Peer-to-Peer Support and Social Media," *Epidemiology and Psychiatric Sciences* 25, no. 2 (2016): 113–22, doi.org/10.1017/S2045796015001067, text available at https://www.ncbi.nlm.nih.gov/pmc/articles/PMC4830464/.

9. Eilis McCaughan, Kader Parahoo, Irene Hueter, Laurel Northouse, and Ian Bradbury, "Online Support Groups for Women with Breast Cancer," *Cochrane Database of Systematic Reviews* 3, no. 3 (2017): CD011652, https:// doi.org/10.1002/14651858.CD011652.pub2.

10. Erica J. Boothby, Margaret S. Clark, and John A. Bargh, "Shared Experiences Are Amplified," *Psychological Science* 25, no. 12 (2014): 2209–16, doi:10.1177/0956797614551162, text available at https://www.researchgate.net/ publication/266570345_Shared_Experiences_Are_Amplified.

11. Alexis Elder, "Excellent Online Friendships: An Aristotelian Defense of Social Media," *Ethics and Information Technology* 16 (2014): 287–97, doi:10.1007/s10676-014-9354-5.

12. Boothby, Clark, and Bargh, "Shared Experiences Are Amplified."

13. Donald Woods Winnicott, "The Theory of the Parent-Infant Relationship," *The International Journal of Psycho-analysis* 41 (1960): 585–95.

14. Priscilla Fishler, Michael Sperling, and Arthur Carr, "Assessment of Adult Relatedness: A Review of Empirical Findings from Object Relations and Attachment Theories," *Journal of Personality Assessment* 55, no. 3 (1990): 499–520, doi:10.1207/s15327752jpa5503&4_9.

15. Shawn M. Burn, "Six Hallmarks of Codependence," *Psychology Today*, April 27, 2016, https://www.psychologytoday.com/us/blog/presence-mind/201604/six-hallmarks-codependence.

16. Melody Beattie, *Codependent No More: How to Stop Controlling Others and Start Caring for Yourself* (New York: Harper/Hazelden, 1986).

17. Kevin J. Yurasek, "Social Media Use during the College Transition" (master's thesis, University of South Florida, 2014), text available at https://scholarcommons.usf.edu/cgi/viewcontent.cgi?article=6356&context=etd.

18. Gregory M. Walton et al., "Mere Belonging: The Power of Social Connections," *Journal of Personality and Social Psychology* 102, no. 3 (2012): 513–32, doi: 10.1037/a0025731, text available at https://pdfs.semanticscholar.org/7d68/1f08ca9b60c3af6fedeff0f49dcf728120c7.pdf?_ga=2.259116746.134741604.1584054368-1598740557.1583881898.

9. BALANCING THE VIRTUAL AND THE ACTUAL LIFE

1. Aristotle, *The Ethics of Aristotle: The Nicomachean Ethics*, trans. James Alexander Kerr Thomson, I:9 (Baltimore: Penguin Books, 1963), 44.

2. Jory MacKay, "Screen Time Stats 2019: Here's How Much You Use Your Phone during the Workday," *RescueTime Blog*, March 21, 2019, https://blog.rescuetime.com/screen-time-stats-2018/.

3. Zagorski, "Using Many Social Media Platforms"; Hui-Tzu G. Chou and Nicholas Edge, "'They Are Happier and Having Better Lives than I Am': The Impact of Using Facebook on Perceptions of Others' Lives," *Cyberpsychology, Behavior, and Social Networking* 15, no. 2 (2012): 117–21, doi:10.1089/cyber.2011.0324.

4. Catherine Price, "Putting Down Your Phone May Help You Live Longer," *New York Times*, April 24, 2019, https://www.nytimes.com/2019/04/24/well/mind/putting-down-your-phone-may-help-you-live-longer.html.

5. International Psychoanalytical Association, "Episode 19: A Psychoanalyst Studies the Good Life—The Harvard Study of Adult Development," *Off the Couch* (podcast), September 21, 2019, http://ipaoffthecouch.org/2019/09/21/episode-19-a-psychoanalyst-studies-the-good-life-the-harvard-study-of-adult-development/.

6. Diana Bruk, "Is 'Phubbing' Ruining Your Relationship?" *Best Life* (blog), October 11, 2018, https://bestlifeonline.com/phubbing/.

7. Adrian Meier, Leonard Reinecke, and Christine E. Meltzer, "'Facebocrastination'? Predictors of Using Facebook for Procrastination and Its Effects

on Students' Well-Being," *Computers in Human Behavior* 64 (2016): 65–76, doi:10.1016/j.chb.2016.06.011.

8. Ludovic S. Mure et al., "Why Screen Time Can Disrupt Sleep," Salk Institute for Biological Studies, November 27, 2018, https://www.salk.edu/news-release/why-screen-time-can-disrupt-sleep/.

9. Allen M. Siegel, *Heinz Kohut and the Psychology of the Self* (London: Routledge, 2008).

10. Tina H. Boogren, *Take Time for You: Self-Care Action Plans for Educators* (Bloomington, IN: Solution Tree Press, 2018).

11. James Hamblin, "Don't Be Surprised If Your Doctor Prescribes a Park," *The Atlantic*, October 2015, https://www.theatlantic.com/magazine/archive/2015/10/the-nature-cure/403210/.

12. Mike Oppland, "8 Ways to Create Flow According to Mihaly Csikszentmihalyi," PositivePsychology.com, November 20, 2019, https://positivepsychology.com/mihaly-csikszentmihalyi-father-of-flow/.

13. Harvard Health Publishing, "12 Ways to Keep Your Brain Young," Harvard Medical School, updated January 29, 2020, https://www.health.harvard.edu/mind-and-mood/12-ways-to-keep-your-brain-young.

SELECTED BIBLIOGRAPHY

Ainsworth, Mary D. Salter, Mary C. Blehar, Everett Waters, and Sally Wall. *Patterns of Attachment: A Psychological Study of the Strange Situation*. Hillsdale, NJ: Erlbaum, 1978.

Akers, Michael, and Grover Porter. "What Is Emotional Intelligence (EQ)?" *Psych Central*. Last modified October 8, 2018. https://psychcentral.com/lib/what-is-emotional-intelligence-eq/.

American Psychological Association. "APA's Survey Finds Constantly Checking Electronic Devices Linked to Significant Stress for Most Americans." APA.org. February 23, 2017. https://www.apa.org/news/press/releases/2017/02/checking-devices.

———. "Connected and Content: Managing Healthy Technology Use." APA.org. 2017. https://www.apa.org/helpcenter/connected-content.

———. "What Is Cognitive Behavioral Therapy?" Clinical Practice Guideline for the Treatment of Posttraumatic Stress Disorder. APA.org. Accessed January 29, 2020. https://www.apa.org/ptsd-guideline/patients-and-families/cognitive-behavioral.

Amsel, Beverly. "The Effects of Parental Involvement on Self-Confidence and Self-Esteem." *GoodTherapy* (blog) July 16, 2013. https://www.goodtherapy.org/blog/effects-of-parental-involvement-on-self-confidence-and-self-esteem-0716134.

Aristotle. *The Ethics of Aristotle: The Nicomachean Ethics*. Translated by James Alexander Kerr Thomson. Baltimore: Penguin Books, 1963.

Auchincloss, Elizabeth L., Eslee Samberg, and the American Psychoanalytic Association. *Psychoanalytic Terms and Concepts*. New Haven, CT: Yale University Press, 2012.

Bartholomew, Kim. "Avoidance of Intimacy: An Attachment Perspective." *Journal of Social and Personal Relationships*. 7, no. 2 (1990): 147–78.

Baumeister, Roy F., and Mark R. Leary. "The Need to Belong: Desire for Interpersonal Attachments as a Fundamental Human Motivation." *Psychological Bulletin* 117, no. 3 (1995): 497–529. doi:10.1037/0033-2909.117.3.497.

Beattie, Melody. *Codependent No More: How to Stop Controlling Others and Start Caring for Yourself*. New York: Harper Hazelden, 1986.

Bergland, Christopher. "Face-to-Face Social Contact Reduces Risk of Depression." *Psychology Today*, October 5, 2015. https://www.psychologytoday.com/us/blog/the-athletes-way/201510/face-face-social-contact-reduces-risk-depression.

Boogren, Tina H. *Take Time for You: Self-Care Action Plans for Educators*. Bloomington, IN: Solution Tree Press, 2018.

Boothby, Erica J., Margaret S. Clark, and John A. Bargh. "Shared Experiences Are Amplified." *Psychological Science* 25, no. 12 (2014): 2209–16. doi:10.1177/0956797614551162. Text available at https://www.researchgate.net/publication/266570345_Shared_Experiences_Are_Amplified.

Bose, Jonaki, Sarra L. Hedden, Rachel N. Lipari, and Eunice Park-Lee. *Key Substance Use and Mental Health Indicators in the United States: Results from the 2017 National Survey on Drug Use and Health.* HHS Publication No. SMA 18-5068, NSDUH Series H-53. Rockville, MD: Center for Behavioral Health Statistics and Quality, Substance Abuse and Mental Health Services Administration, 2018. https://www.samhsa.gov/data/sites/default/files/cbhsq-reports/NSDUHFFR2017/NSDUHFFR2017.htm.

Bowlby, John. *A Secure Base: Clinical Applications of Attachment Theory.* London: Routledge, 2005.

———. *Attachment and Loss.* Vol. 1, *Attachment.* New York: Basic Books, 1969.

———. *Attachment and Loss.* Vol. 2, *Separation: Anxiety and Anger.* New York: Basic Books, 1973.

———. *Attachment and Loss.* Vol. 3, *Loss.* New York: Basic Books, 1980.

Breines, Juliana G., and Serena Chen. "Self-Compassion Increases Self-Improvement Motivation." *Personality and Social Psychology Bulletin* 38, no. 9 (2012): 1133–43. doi:10.1177/0146167212445599.

Bruk, Diana. "Is 'Phubbing' Ruining Your Relationship?" *Best Life* (blog), October 11, 2018. https://bestlifeonline.com/phubbing/.

Buote, Vanessa M., Eileen Wood, and Michael Pratt. "Exploring Similarities and Differences between Online and Offline Friendships: The Role of Attachment Style." *Computers in Human Behavior* 25, no. 2 (2009): 560–67. https://doi.org/10.1016/j.chb.2008.12.022.

Burn, Shawn M. "Six Hallmarks of Codependence." *Psychology Today.* April 27, 2016. https://www.psychologytoday.com/us/blog/presence-mind/201604/six-hallmarks-codependence.

Carrilio, Terry E., and Carolyn A. Walter. "Mirroring and Autonomy: The Dual Tasks of Mothers." *Child & Adolescent Social Work Journal* 1, no. 3 (1984): 143–52. doi:10.1007/bf00798430.

Chou, Hui-Tzu G., and Nicholas Edge. "'They Are Happier and Having Better Lives than I Am': The Impact of Using Facebook on Perceptions of Others' Lives." *Cyberpsychology, Behavior, and Social Networking* 15, no. 2 (2012): 117–21. doi:10.1089/cyber.2011.0324.

Csikszentmihalyi, Mihaly. *Flow: The Psychology of Optimal Experience.* New York: HarperCollins, 2009.

Cui, Guoqiang. "Evaluating Online Social Presence: An Overview of Social Presence Assessment." *Journal of Educational Technology Development and Exchange* 6, no. 1 (2013). doi:10.18785/jetde.0601.02.

Daft, Richard L., and Robert H. Lengel. "Organizational Information Requirements, Media Richness and Structural Design." *Management Science* 32, no. 5 (1986): 554–71. doi:10.1287/mnsc.32.5.554.

Dalai Lama XIV and Howard C. Cutler. *The Art of Happiness: A Handbook for Living.* Norwalk, CT: Easton Press, 1998.

D'Arienzo, Maria C., Valentina Boursier, and Mark D. Griffiths. "Addiction to Social Media and Attachment Styles: A Systematic Literature Review." *International Journal of Mental Health and Addiction* 17, no. 4 (2019): 1094–18. doi:10.1007/s11469-019-00082-5.

Deloitte. *2018 Global Mobile Consumer Survey: US Edition; A New Era in Mobile Continues.* New York: Deloitte Development, LLC, 2018. https://www2.deloitte.com/content/dam/Deloitte/us/Documents/technology-media-telecommunications/us-tmt-global-mobile-consumer-survey-exec-summary-2018.pdf.

Dogan, Volkan. "Why Do People Experience the Fear of Missing Out (FoMO)? Exposing the Link Between the Self and the FoMO through Self-Construal." *Journal of Cross-Cultural Psychology* 50, no. 4 (2019): 524–38. doi:10.1177/0022022119839145.

Eating Disorders Coalition. "Facts about Eating Disorders: What the Research Shows." Accessed January 29, 2020. http://eatingdisorderscoalition.org.s208556.gridserver.com/couch/uploads/file/fact-sheet_2016.pdf.

Eckel, Sara. "The Power of Boundaries." *Psychology Today*, October 14, 2019. https://www.psychologytoday.com/us/articles/201910/the-power-boundaries.

Elder, Alexis. "Excellent Online Friendships: An Aristotelian Defense of Social Media." *Ethics and Information Technology* 16, no. 4 (2014): 287–97. doi:10.1007/s10676-014-9354-5.

Ellis, Albert, and Windy Dryden. *The Practice of Rational Emotive Behavior Therapy: Second Edition.* New York: Springer Publishing Company, 2007.

Emmons, Robert A. *Thanks: How Practicing Gratitude Can Make You Happier.* Boston: Houghton Mifflin Harcourt, 2008.

Erikson, Erik H. *Childhood and Society.* New York: W. W. Norton & Company, 1950.

Fardouly, Jasmine, and Lenny R. Vartanian. "Negative Comparisons about One's Appearance Mediate the Relationship between Facebook Usage and Body Image Concerns." *Body Image* 12 (2015): 82–88. doi:10.1016/j.bodyim.2014.10.004.

Festinger, Leon. "A Theory of Social Comparison Processes." *Human Relations* 7, no. 2 (1954): 117–40. doi:10.1177/001872675400700202.

Fishler, Priscilla, Michael Sperling, and Arthur Carr. "Assessment of Adult Relatedness: A Review of Empirical Findings from Object Relations and Attachment Theories." *Journal of Personality Assessment* 55, no. 3 (1990): 499–520. doi:10.1207/s15327752jpa5503&4_9.

Fiske, Susan T. "Envy Up, Scorn Down: How Comparison Divides Us." *American Psychologist* 65, no. 8 (2010): 698–706. doi:10.1037/0003-066x.65.8.698.

Frankl, Viktor E. *Man's Search for Meaning: An Introduction to Logotherapy*, 4th ed. Preface by Gordon W. Allport. Boston: Beacon Press, 1992.

Freud, Sigmund. *Letters of Sigmund Freud, 1873–1939.* Edited by Ernst L. Freud, translated by Tania Stern and James Stern. London: Hogarth Press, 1960, 1961.

Gallagher, Matthew W. "Introduction to Positive Psychological Assessment." In *Positive Psychological Assessment: A Handbook of Models and Measures*, 2nd ed., edited by Matthew W. Gallagher and Shane J. Lopez, 3–9. Washington, DC: American Psychological Association, 2019. doi:10.1037/0000138-001. https://www.apa.org/pubs/books/Ch1-Sample-Positive-Psychological-Assessment-Second-Edition-Sample.pdf.

Germer, Christopher K., and Kristin D. Neff. "Self-Compassion in Clinical Practice." *Journal of Clinical Psychology* 69, no. 8 (2013): 856–67. doi:10.1002/jclp.22021.

Gilbert, Paul, and Chris Irons. "Compassion Focused Therapy." In *The Beginner's Guide to Counselling & Psychotherapy*, edited by Stephen Palmer, 127–39. London: Routledge, 2015.

Grohol, John M. "15 Common Cognitive Distortions." *Psych Central.* Last updated June 24, 2019. https://psychcentral.com/lib/15-common-cognitive-distortions/.

Hamblin, James. "Don't Be Surprised If Your Doctor Prescribes a Park." *The Atlantic*, October 2015. https://www.theatlantic.com/magazine/archive/2015/10/the-nature-cure/403210/.

Harvard Health Publishing. "Can Relationships Boost Longevity and Well-being?" *Harvard Health Letter.* Last modified September 24, 2019. https://webcache.googleusercontent.com/search?q=cache:h126n1Jd7FYJ:https://www.health.harvard.edu/mental-health/can-relationships-boost-longevity-and-well-being+&cd=1&hl=en&ct=clnk&gl=us&client=safari.

———. "12 Ways to Keep Your Brain Young." Harvard Medical School. Updated January 29, 2020. https://www.health.harvard.edu/mind-and-mood/12-ways-to-keep-your-brain-young.

Holt-Lunstad, Julianne, Timothy B. Smith, and J. B. Layton. "Social Relationships and Mortality Risk: A Meta-analytic Review." *PLoS Medicine* 7, no. 7 (2010): e1000316. doi:10.1371/journal.pmed.1000316. https://journals.plos.org/plosmedicine/article?id=10.1371/journal.pmed.1000316.

International Psychoanalytical Association. "Episode 19: A Psychoanalyst Studies the Good Life—The Harvard Study of Adult Development." *Off the Couch* (podcast). September 21, 2019. http://ipaoffthecouch.org/2019/09/21/episode-19-a-psychoanalyst-studies-the-good-life-the-harvard-study-of-adult-development/.

Khoshaba, Deborah. "About Complicated Bereavement Disorder." *Psychology Today*, September 28, 2013. https://www.psychologytoday.com/us/blog/get-hardy/201309/about-complicated-bereavement-disorder-0.

Klein, Melanie. *The Writings of Melanie Klein.* Vol. 3, *Envy and Gratitude and Other Works, 1946–1963.* London: Hogarth Press, 1975.

Knight, Zelda G. "The Use of the 'Corrective Emotional Experience' and the Search for the Bad Object in Psychotherapy." *American Journal of Psychotherapy* 59, no. 1 (2005): 30–41. doi:10.1176/appi.psychotherapy.2005.59.1.30.

Kohut, Heinz. *The Psychology of the Self: A Casebook.* Madison, WI: International Universities Press, 1992.

Kraut, Richard. "Aristotle's Ethics." *The Stanford Encyclopedia of Philosophy,* Summer 2018 edition. Accessed January 15, 2020. https://plato.stanford.edu/entries/aristotle-ethics/.

Kübler-Ross, Elisabeth, and David Kessler. *On Grief and Grieving: Finding the Meaning of Grief through the Five Stages of Loss.* New York: Simon & Schuster, 2005.

Laurenceaum, Jean-Philippe, Paula R. Pietromonaco, and Lisa Feldman Barrett. "Intimacy as an Interpersonal Process: The Importance of Self-Disclosure, Partner Disclosure, and Perceived Partner Responsiveness in Interpersonal Exchanges." *Journal of Personality and Social Psychology* 74, no. 5 (1998): 1238–51. https://www.researchgate.net/profile/Lisa_Barrett3/publication/13685624_Intima-cy_as_an_Interpersonal_Process_the_Importance_of_Self-Disclo-sure_Partner_Disclosure_and_Perceived_Partner_Responsiveness_in_Interpersonal_Exchanges/links/0c960517a6ba3a7f28000000.pdf.

Lemieux, Robert, Sean Lajoie, and Nathan E. Trainor. "Affinity-Seeking, Social Loneliness, and Social Avoidance among Facebook Users." *Psychological Reports* 112, no. 2 (2013): 545–52. doi:10.2466/07.pr0.112.2.545-552.

Lin, Liu Yi, Jaime E. Sidani, Ariel Shensa, Ana Radovic, Elizabeth Miller, Jason B. Colditz, Beth L. Hoffman, Leila M. Giles, and Brian A. Primack. "Association between Social Media Use and Depression among U.S. Young Adults." *Depression and Anxiety* 33, no. 4 (2016): 323–31. doi:10.1002/da.22466. https://www.ncbi.nlm.nih.gov/pmc/articles/PMC4853817/.

Linehan, Marsha M. *Cognitive-Behavioral Treatment of Borderline Personality Disorder.* New York: Guilford Publications, 2018.

Lipari, Rachel N., Eunice Park-Le, and Substance Abuse and Mental Health Services Administration (SAMHSA). *Key Substance Use and Mental Health Indicators in the United States: Results from the 2018 National Survey on Drug Use and Health.* HHS publication no. PEP19-5068, NSDUH Series H-54. Rockville, MD: Center for Behavioral Health Statistics and Quality, Substance Abuse and Mental Health Services Administration, 2019. https://www.samhsa.gov/data/sites/default/files/cbhsq-reports/NSDUHNationalFindings-Report2018/NSDUHNationalFindingsReport2018.pdf.

MacKay, Jory. "Screen Time Stats 2019: Here's How Much You Use Your Phone during the Workday." *RescueTime Blog.* March 21, 2019. https://blog.rescuetime.com/screen-time-stats-2018/.

Marcel, Gabriel. *The Philosophy of Existence.* Translated by Manya Harari. London: The Harvill Press.

Martos, Cristina Miguel. "The Transformation of Intimacy and Privacy through Social Networking Sites." Paper. Accessed January 27, 2020. Text available at http://pvac-webhost2.leeds.ac.uk/ics/files/2013/07/Miguel_The-Transformation-of-Intimacy-and-Privacy-through-Social-Networking-Sites.pdf.

Maslow, Abraham H. "A Theory of Human Motivation." *Psychological Review* 50 (1943): 370–96. Text available at http://psychclassics.yorku.ca/Maslow/motivation.htm.

———. *Motivation and Personality,* 2nd ed. New York: Aesculapius, 1970.

McCaughan, Eilis, Kader Parahoo, Irene Hueter, Laurel Northouse, and Ian Bradbury. "Online Support Groups for Women with Breast Cancer." *Cochrane Database of Systematic Reviews* 3, no. 3 (2017): CD011652. https://doi.org/10.1002/14651858.CD011652.pub2.

McLeod, Saul. "Maslow's Hierarchy of Needs." *Simply Psychology.* Last modified 2018. https://www.simplypsychology.org/maslow.html.

Meier, Adrian, Leonard Reinecke, and Christine E. Meltzer. "'Facebocrastination'? Predictors of Using Facebook for Procrastination and Its Effects on Students' Well-Being." *Computers in Human Behavior* 64 (2016): 65–76. doi:10.1016/j.chb.2016.06.011.

Merriam-Webster. S.v. "Envy." Accessed January 26, 2020. https://www.merriam-webster.com/dictionary/envy.

Miguel, Cristina. "Visual Intimacy on Social Media: From Selfies to the Co-construction of Intimacies through Shared Pictures." *Social Media + Society* 2, no. 2 (2016): 205630511664170. doi:10.1177/2056305116641705. https://journals.sagepub.com/doi/10.1177/2056305116641705.

Mure, Ludovic S., Megumi Hatori, Kiersten Ruda, Giorgia Benegiamo, James Demas, and Satchidananda Panda. "Why Screen Time Can Disrupt Sleep." Salk Institute for Biological Studies. November 27, 2018. https://www.salk.edu/news-release/why-screen-time-can-disrupt-sleep/.

Naslund, John A., Kelly A. Aschbrenner, Lisa A. Marsch, and Stephen J. Bartels. "The Future of Mental Health Care: Peer-to-Peer Support and Social Media." *Epidemiology and Psychiatric Sciences* 25, no. 2 (2016): 113–22. doi.org/10.1017/S2045796015001067. Text available at https://www.ncbi.nlm.nih.gov/pmc/articles/PMC4830464/

Neff, Kristin. "Definition of Self-Compassion." *Self-Compassion*. Last modified March 22, 2011. https://self-compassion.org/the-three-elements-of-self-compassion-2.

Nielsen. "Time Flies: U.S. Adults Now Spend Nearly Half a Day Interacting with Media." July 31, 2018. https://www.nielsen.com/en/insights/article/2018/time-flies-us-adults-now-spend-nearly-half-a-day-interacting-with-media/.

O'Connor, Joseph, and Andrea Lages. "Thinking about Change: Neuroplasticity." In *Coaching the Brain: Practical Applications of Neuroscience to Coaching*, 17–29. London: Routledge, 2019. doi:10.4324/9780203733370-3.

Oldmeadow, Julian A., Sally Quinn, and Rachel Kowert. "Attachment Style, Social Skills, and Facebook Use amongst Adults." *Computers in Human Behavior* 29, no. 3 (2013): 1142–49. doi: 10.1016/j.chb.2012.10.006.

Oppland, Mike. "8 Ways to Create Flow According to Mihaly Csikszentmihalyi." PositivePsychology.com. November 20, 2019. https://positivepsychology.com/mihaly-csikszentmihalyi-father-of-flow/.

Pederson, Lane. *The DBT Deck for Clients and Therapists: 101 Mindful Practices to Manage Distress, Regulate Emotions & Build Better Relationships*. Eau Claire, WI: PESI Publishing, 2019.

Perloff, Richard M. "Social Media Effects on Young Women's Body Image Concerns: Theoretical Perspectives and an Agenda for Research." *Sex Roles* 71, nos. 11–12 (2014): 363–77. doi:10.1007/s11199-014-0384-6. https://www.researchgate.net/publication/271740741_Social_Media_Effects_on_Young_Women's_Body_Image_Concerns_Theoretical_Perspectives_and_an_Agenda_for_Research.

Petersen, Andrea. "As Suicides Rise, More Attention Turns to the People Left Behind." *Wall Street Journal*, December 2, 2019. https://www.wsj.com/articles/as-suicides-rise-more-attention-turns-to-the-people-left-behind-11575282602 (paywall).

Petersen, Neil. "How Social Media Influences Offline Behavior." *AllPsych* (blog). March 31, 2017. https://blog.allpsych.com/how-social-media-influences-offline-behavior/.

Pew Research Center. "Social Media Fact Sheet." Internet & Technology. June 12, 2019. https://www.pewresearch.org/internet/fact-sheet/social-media/.

Price, Catherine. "Putting Down Your Phone May Help You Live Longer." *New York Times*, April 24, 2019. https://www.nytimes.com/2019/04/24/well/mind/putting-down-your-phone-may-help-you-live-longer.html.

Psychology Today. "Relational Therapy." Accessed January 20, 2020. https://www.psychologytoday.com/us/therapy-types/relational-therapy.

Santarossa, Sara, and Sarah J. Woodruff. "#SocialMedia: Exploring the Relationship of Social Networking Sites on Body Image, Self-Esteem, and Eating Disorders." *Social Media + Society* 3, no. 2 (2017): 205630511770440. doi:10.1177/2056305117704407. https://journals.sagepub.com/doi/full/10.1177/2056305117704407.

Sarkis, Stephanie A. "11 Warning Signs of Gaslighting." *Psychology Today*. January 22, 2017. https://www.psychologytoday.com/us/blog/here-there-and-everywhere/201701/11-warning-signs-gaslighting.

Savelle-Rocklin, Nina, and Salman Akhtar. *Beyond the Primal Addiction: Food, Sex, Gambling, Internet, Shopping, and Work*. London: Routledge, 2019.

Segal, Hanna. *Introduction to the Work of Melanie Klein*. London: Routledge, 2018.

Shiller, Virginia M. *The Attachment Bond: Affectional Ties across the Lifespan*. Lanham, MD: Lexington Books, 2017.

Siegel, Allen M. *Heinz Kohut and the Psychology of the Self*. London: Routledge, 2008.

Sinclair, Vaughn G., and Sharon W. Dowdy. "Development and Validation of the Emotional Intimacy Scale." *Journal of Nursing Measurement* 13, no. 3 (2005): 193–206. doi:10.1891/jnum.13.3.193.

Sreenivasan, Shoba, and Linda E. Weinberger. "Why We Need Each Other." *Psychology Today*. December 14, 2016. https://www.psychologytoday.com/us/blog/emotional-nourishment/201612/why-we-need-each-other.

Thompson, J. Kevin, and Eric Stice. "Thin-Ideal Internalization: Mounting Evidence for a New Risk Factor for Body-Image Disturbance and Eating Pathology." *Current Directions in Psychological Science* 10, no. 5 (2001): 181–83. doi:10.1111/1467-8721.00144.

Tolstoy, Leo. "Some Social Remedies: Three Methods of Reform." In *Pamphlets*. Christchurch, Hants.: The Free Age Press, 1900.

Turkle, Sherry. *Alone Together: Why We Expect More from Technology and Less from Each Other*. New York: Basic Books, 2017.

US National Library of Medicine. "Mental Health." *MedlinePlus*. Last modified December 3, 2019. https://medlineplus.gov/mentalhealth.html.

van den Berg, Patricia, J. Kevin Thompson, Karen Obremski-Brandon, and Michael Coovert. "The Tripartite Influence Model of Body Image and Eating Disturbance." *Journal of Psychosomatic Research* 53, no. 5 (2002): 1007–20. doi:10.1016/s0022-3999(02)00499-3.

van den Eijnden, Regina J. J. M., Jeroen S. Lemmens, and Patti M. Valkenburg. "The Social Media Disorder Scale." *Computers in Human Behavior* 61 (2016): 478–87. doi:10.1016/j.chb.2016.03.038. https://www.sciencedirect.com/science/article/pii/S0747563216302059.

van Deursen, Alexander Johannes Aloysius Maria, and Petrus A. M. Kommers. "Modeling Habitual and Addictive Smartphone Behavior: The Role of Smartphone Usage Types, Emotional Intelligence, Social Stress, Self-Regulation, Age, and Gender." *Computers in Human Behavior* 45 (2015): 411–20. doi:10.1016/j.chb.2014.12.039.

Verduyn, Philippe, David S. Lee, Jiyoung Park, Holly Shablack, Ariana Orvell, Joseph Bayer, Oscar Ybarra, John Jonides, and Ethan Kross. "Passive Facebook Usage Undermines Affective Well-Being: Experimental and Longitudinal Evidence." *Journal of Experimental Psychology: General* 144, no. 2 (2015): 480–88. doi:10.1037/xge0000057.

Verheugt-Pleiter, Annelies, and Margit Deben-Mager. "Transference-Focused Psychotherapy and Mentalization-Based Treatment: Brother and Sister?" *Psychoanalytic Psychotherapy* 20, no. 4 (2006): 297–315. doi:10.1080/02668730601020374.

Walton, Gregory M., Geoffrey L. Cohen, David Cwir, and Steven John Spencer. "Mere Belonging: The Power of Social Connections." *Journal of Personality and Social Psychology* 102, no. 3 (2012): 513–32. doi: 10.1037/a0025731. Text available at https://pdfs.semanticscholar.org/7d68/1f08ca9b60c3af6fedeff0f49dcf728120c7.pdf?_ga=2.259116746.134741604.1584054368-1598740557.1583881898Weiler, Nicholas.

Weiler, Nicholas. "Protein Links Alcohol Abuse and Changes in Brain's Reward Center." UC San Francisco. September 7, 2017. https://www.ucsf.edu/news/2017/09/408236/protein-links-alcohol-abuse-and-changes-brains-reward-center.

Wharton, Edith. "Vesalius in Zante. (1564)." *North American Review* 175, no. 552 (Nov. 1902): 625–31. Text available at https://public.wsu.edu/~campbelld/wharton/whartpoe2.htm#Vesalius%20in%20Zante.%20(1564).

Wikipedia. S.v. "Media Literacy." Last modified March 9, 2020. https://en.wikipedia.org/wiki/Media_literacy.

Winnicott, Donald Woods. "The Theory of the Parent-Infant Relationship." *The International Journal of Psycho-analysis* 41 (1960): 585–95.

Yurasek, Kevin J. "Social Media Use during the College Transition." Master's thesis, University of South Florida, 2014. Text available at https://scholarcommons.usf.edu/cgi/viewcontent.cgi?article=6356&context=etd.

Zagorski, Nick. "Using Many Social Media Platforms Linked with Depression, Anxiety Risk." *Psychiatric News* 52, no. 2 (2017): 1. doi:10.1176/appi.pn.2017.1b16. Text available at https://psychnews.psychiatryonline.org/doi/full/10.1176/appi.pn.2017.1b16.

INDEX

ABOUT THE AUTHOR

Paula Durlofsky, PhD, is a licensed psychologist with a private practice in Bryn Mawr, Pennsylvania. As a practicing therapist for over eighteen years and recently declared best therapist in 2017's Best of the Main Line awards, Dr. Durlofsky helps individuals, couples, and families reach their full potential for leading lives with passion and purpose. Dr. Durlofsky is a member of the American Psychological Association's Device Management and Digital Intelligence Committee, whose goal is to support healthy relationships with technology through intelligent engagement and modeling positive digital citizenship. She is also affiliated with Bryn Mawr Hospital, Lankenau Medical Center, and the Psychoanalytic Center of Philadelphia. Over the course of her career, she has taught as adjunct professor and instructor to medical residents specializing in internal medicine and psychiatry. She has even been immortalized as the inspiration for the character Dr. Paula Agard on the popular USA Network show *Suits*. Dr. Durlofsky has been writing professionally since 2012. Her expert opinions based on over two decades of clinical experience and training have been featured in *Marie Claire*, *Teen Vogue*, the APA's *Monitor on Psychology*, *Exceptional Parent* magazine, *Main Line Health*, *Psych Central*, and *Main Line Today*, as well as at the Pennsylvania Conference for Women and on ABC 10-KXTV.